Galilee Divided

Westview Special Studies

The concept of Westview Special Studies is a response to the continuing crisis in academic and informational publishing. Library budgets are being diverted from the purchase of books and used for data banks, computers, micromedia, and other methods of information retrieval. Interlibrary loan structures further reduce the edition sizes required to satisfy the needs of the scholarly community. Economic pressures on university presses and the few private scholarly publishing companies have greatly limited the capacity of the industry to properly serve the academic and research communities. As a result, many manuscripts dealing with important subjects, often representing the highest level of scholarship, are no longer economically viable publishing projects--or, if accepted for publication, are typically subject to lead times ranging from one to three years.

Westview Special Studies are our practical solution to the problem. As always, the selection criteria include the importance of the subject, the work's contribution to scholarship, and its insight, originality of thought, and excellence of exposition. We accept manuscripts in camera-ready form, typed, set, or word processed according to specifications laid out in our comprehensive manual, which contains straightforward instructions and sample pages. The responsibility for editing and proofreading lies with the author or sponsoring institution, but our editorial staff is always available to answer questions and provide guidance.

The result is a book printed on acid-free paper and bound in sturdy, library-quality soft covers. We manufacture these books ourselves using equipment that does not require a lengthy make-ready process and that allows us to publish first editions of 300 to 1000 copies and to reprint even smaller quantities as needed. Thus, we can produce Special Studies quickly and can keep even very specialized books in print as long as there is a demand for them.

About the Book and Author

Security problems associated with the Lebanon-Palestine/Israel frontier have arisen periodically ever since France and Great Britain partitioned Galilee in the wake of World War I. This study analyzes the complexities of Lebanese-Israeli interaction along their common border both chronologically and functionally. The author begins by examining the initial partition of Galilee between the two Levantine states and its immediate consequences. He then considers the evolution of the two basic problems not resolved by Great Britain and France with regard to the frontier: water and security. Later chapters focus on the manner in which southern Lebanon became the focal point of the Arab-Israeli confrontation, the attendant destruction of the Lebanese state, and the aborted May 1983 Israel-Lebanon agreement. The author concludes that there will be no peace for Galilee without a real government for Lebanon.

Frederic C. Hof is a U.S. Army officer who has spent most of his sixteen-year career in assignments and training related to the Middle East. He recently served on the staff of the Long Commission, which investigated the October 1983 bombing of the Marine barracks at Beirut International Airport.

Galilee Divided
The Israel-Lebanon Frontier, 1916–1984

Frederic C. Hof
Foreword by Philip C. Habib

Westview Press / Boulder and London

Westview Special Studies on the Middle East

Copyright © 1985 by Westview Press, Inc.

Published in 1985 in the United States of America by Westview Press, Inc.;
Frederick A. Praeger, Publisher; 5500 Central Avenue, Boulder, Colorado 80301

Library of Congress Cataloging in Publication Data
Hof, Frederic C.
    Galilee divided.
    (Westview special studies on the Middle East)
    Bibliography: p.
    1. Israel--Boundaries--Lebanon. 2. Lebanon--
Boundaries--Israel. I. Title. II. Series.
DS119.8.L4H64 1984   956.92   85-3291
ISBN 0-8133-0189-0

Composition for this book was provided by the author
Printed and bound in the United States of America

10 9 8 7 6 5 4 3 2 1

Contents

Figures

Foreword

The threat of conflict in the Middle East remains a critical issue affecting U.S. interests. In recent years, the Israel/Lebanon border has been one of the hot spots across which such hostilities have occasionally erupted. The Israelis have entered Lebanon on a number of occasions, the most dramatic instance being in 1982. The border area remains of critical concern to the peoples of the region and continues to be an unresolved problem capable of recreating additional crises in the future. LTC Hof's book treats the Israel/Lebanon border in both its historical and current perspectives and amply illustrates the fragility of the current situation by shedding light on past disputes and on the potential for future differences. What emerges is a clear demonstration of the need for a process that deals with the larger issues in order to avoid disturbances that can arise from particular situations. Here, the larger issue of the search for peace in the face of the long-standing Arab/Israeli conflict remains paramount. The problems along the Israel/Lebanon border are magnified by the failure to meet the needs of the overriding problem, and hostilities in the border region are a direct consequence of the inability to come to grips with the longer-term issues. This creates the dismal prospect that we have not seen the last of the crises along and across the demarcation line. To the extent that such crises arise, they draw attention away from the larger problem and interfere with the revitalization of the peace process. In the final analysis, that is the most important consequence of instability in the border area. The background for our understanding of this larger problem is immeasurably increased by the careful research and thoughtful analysis contained in this book.

Philip C. Habib

Preface

Ten years have passed since the independent Lebanese state, born in 1943, died violently in the streets of downtown Beirut. Alive, Lebanon was too weak and militarily inconsequential to be categorized as a "confrontation state" in the Arab-Israeli context; this, despite the existence of a common border with Israel. Yet, dead, Lebanon was drawn into the very center of the Arab-Israeli vortex, an abyss from which it has yet to emerge.

Hindsight enables us to see clearly now that the glitter and glamor of Beirut in the 1960s was but a facade which masked an ugliness perceived by very few. How obvious it now seems that the Grand Liban created by France in 1920, the unnatural offspring of French imperialism and Christian Lebanese nationalism, was born to die the way it did. How incongruous it now seems that the savage primordialism of Lebanon's sectarian communities, an ever-present condition brought rapidly into the open by the ferocity of the Palestinian-Zionist confrontation, lay hidden for years at a time. How tragic it is that the Lebanese people, whose extraordinary talents and charm make them the most prized of immigrants in many lands, were unable to grace their own beautiful country with a government dedicated to the welfare and protection of all. It was this failure, the product of incredibly short-sighted localism, confessionalism, and greed, which fumbled the fate of Lebanon itself into non-Lebanese hands. Foreigners, whether buying the services of Lebanese journalists and gunmen or occupying Lebanese land, found this fragmented society to be penetrable everywhere and in all respects.

Nowhere was the absence of a state felt more keenly than in the impoverished districts of the south. This was (and is) an area populated mainly by Muslims of the Shi'a sect, Lebanon's poorest group and today its most populous. They occupy, among other places, the northern portion of Upper Galilee, a hilly region divided in 1920 by Great Britain and France between two new political entities: Palestine and Lebanon. From the very beginning the two client groups--Zionists and Christian Lebanese nationalists--standing behind the imperial powers had sharply differing appraisals of Upper Galilee's utility. By 1920 the Zionists had already formulated plans for the exploitation of Galilee's water resources, and lobbied long and hard for

preserving Galilee's unity by placing Palestine's northern
boundary on the Litani River. France's clients, on the other
hand, merely desired an enlarged state which would replicate the
boundaries of a bygone "historic Lebanon." Their interest in the
human and hydrographic potentialities of Upper Galilee was nil.
Indeed, when the Litani River was finally exploited by the
Lebanese government in the 1960s, the main beneficiary was the
capital city with its insatiable appetite for electricity.

Despite their bitter disappointment at losing the northern
districts of Upper Galilee, the Zionists eventually accepted the
legality and finality of Palestine's northern boundary. Yet
southern Lebanon languished under the benign neglect of both
Beirut and its own feudal leaders, and as battle lines were drawn
between Arab and Jew over the possession of Palestine, both the
livelihoods and lives of southern Lebanese became imperiled. The
Lebanese part of Upper Galilee was a security vacuum which, in
1936, 1948, and 1968 filled up with extralegal armed elements
seeking a base from which to strike southward. The creation of
Israel brought, for the first time, the effective closure of the
boundary created just a quarter of a century earlier, thereby
shutting off an economic safety valve which had enabled Lebanese
peasants to seek employment in the prospering districts of
northern Palestine. By the 1970s southern Lebanon had become a
virtual free-fire zone where death and destruction were routine.
In June 1982 Upper Galilee was reunified--temporarily, so it
seemed--under the auspices of the Israel Defense Forces (IDF).

As these words are being written (in late 1984) the Israeli
occupation of southern Lebanon approaches its third year. By all
accounts it is an occupation which Israel finds to be increasingly
difficult, both because of the expense being shouldered by a sick
Israeli economy, as well as the casualty-producing militancy
growing within the Shi'a community. The IDF may well be on the
verge of leaving, but there should be no illusion about the long-
term value of a mere evacuation of occupying military forces. The
research undertaken in writing this volume suggests that there
will be no lasting peace for Galilee--on either side of the
border--without a real government for Lebanon. Six decades worth
of evidence supports this conclusion. Lebanon has never enjoyed
the benefits of a real government, so anything resembling the
resurrection of that which died in 1975 will simply set the stage
for more disaster. If a new Lebanon is to be born in 1985,
however, it will require the cooperation and support of many
Lebanese to whom the leaders of the old regime offered little in
exchange for their votes. The political awakening and
mobilization of Lebanon's Shi'a Muslims suggests that there will
be no real government in Beirut unless it is one which addresses,
at last, the needs of the people living on the Lebanese side of
Galilee divided.

Frederic C. Hof

Acknowledgments

The author accepts full responsibility for the content of this book, but nevertheless wishes to recognize the important contributions made by others.

Dr. Robert De Gross and Commander Bruce Watson of the Defense Intelligence College were most generous in their support of this research project. Mrs. Mary El Qadi of the Armed Forces Staff College provided invaluable editorial assistance, and Professor Kamil Said of the Naval Postgraduate School was most helpful in the drafting stages.

A particular debt of gratitude is owed to Major Harry Klein of the Defense Intelligence Agency. Without his constant prodding this research effort never would have seen the light of day. Major Klein is still remembered in Lebanon as an officer who served the United Nations in the south with distinction, compassion, and courage.

Finally, I wish to thank my wife and children for bearing with me while Lebanon absorbed much of my attention.

F.C.H.

Introduction

On 1 March 1920 a small Jewish outpost located above the northwestern corner of the Hula Valley -- a region claimed by both Great Britain and France, but defended by neither -- was attacked and overwhelmed by a force of Damascus-based Arabs. Joseph Trumpeldor, a well-known Jewish war hero, was killed along with seven others in the defense of Tel Hai. The survivors fled for their lives, and the Jewish residents of Palestine -- an area as yet undefined politically -- angrily demanded that the occupying British military authorities in Jerusalem do something to guarantee the physical security of outlying Jewish settlements. As a result of the incident at Tel Hai, the Hula Valley and lands adjacent to it became northern Palestine instead of southern Lebanon.

Sixty-three years later negotiators representing the states of Lebanon and Israel signed an agreement intended to impose order on the south of Lebanon, a region that had remained, since the days of Tel Hai, virtually ungoverned. The agreement was occasioned by the fact that in June 1982 the martial descendants of the Tel Hai defenders had become the occupiers of southern Lebanon. Although the agreement aimed to terminate that occupation, the Israel Defense Forces remain in control of southern Lebanon as of this writing.

Security problems associated with the Lebanon-Palestine/Israel frontier have arisen periodically ever since France and Great Britain divided the eastern Levant in the wake of World War I. The Israeli invasion of June 1982 and the subsequent Israel-Lebanon agreement seem to have terminated the latest episode of unrest, namely the era of Palestinian military presence in the south of Lebanon. It remains to be seen, however, whether or not the agreement -- or one similar to it -- will ameliorate the conditions which permitted the frontier to become the scene of widespread devastation and bloodshed from mid-1968 through mid-1982. It is this question that forms the basis for the present study.

Is it safe to assume that the demise of the Palestine Liberation Organization as a military force in southern Lebanon

1

signals the beginning of peace and quiet along the Israel-Lebanon border? It would seem that Israel, having named its June 1982 invasion "Operation Peace for Galilee," accepted the assumption as valid. Yet many knowledgeable analysts have concluded that the invasion's real aim was the destruction of the PLO as a political force, an objective more closely tied to developments on the West Bank and the Gaza Strip than to southern Lebanon. Furthermore, no Lebanese government capable of complying with the terms of an agreement with Israel has emerged, raising new doubts about the prospects for an enduring peace. Is it possible that security problems in the Israel-Lebanon frontier region transcend the Israeli-Palestinian confrontation? Could southern Lebanon again become a violent focal point for the concerns of regional actors and superpowers alike?

This study was undertaken on the assumption that an examination of the history of security problems associated with the Lebanon-Palestine/Israel frontier would lead to a better understanding of current conditions. Furthermore it might be possible to uncover frontier problems which have persisted since the inception of the two states, problems which, if not adequately addressed by an adequate Lebanese-Israeli arrangement, can be expected to arise again.

It will be shown in the following pages that several themes run continously through the six-plus decades of the frontier's existence. Some of the more salient are the following: a mild form of Zionist irredentist feeling toward the south of Lebanon; an indifference of the central authorities in Beirut toward the people and resources of southern Lebanon; and a degeneration of the region into a combat zone due to Beirut's political paralysis in the face of Arab-Zionist violence. There are likewise precursors to the 1983 security agreement, namely the 1926 "Good Neighbourly Relations" accord between Palestine, Lebanon, and Syria, and the 1949 Israel-Lebanon General Armistice Agreement. Events, themes, and agreements will all be examined with an eye toward evaluating the 1983 agreement and the prospects for the future of the Israel-Lebanon frontier region.

Although the problems associated with the frontier are anything but a conventional boundary dispute, it will be seen that the way in which the border came into being set the stage for future problems. The study begins, therefore, with an analysis of how it was decided where Palestine would end and Lebanon begin.

1. The Creation of the Palestine-Lebanon Boundary

The current boundary between Israel and Lebanon took its final form in April 1924, when several villages in Upper Galilee were incorporated into Palestine in accordance with the terms of an Anglo-French Convention of March 1923. The presumably simple process of drawing a line between two territorially insignificant states had, in fact, been an extraordinarily arduous endeavor involving the machinations of two major actors and their clients: Great Britain and the Zionists versus France and a group of Christian Lebanese nationalists.

The process began in May 1916 with an exchange of notes between the British Foreign Minister, Sir Edward Grey, and the French Ambassador to the court of St. James, M. Paul Cambon. Later endorsed by Imperial Russia, this provisional arrangement for the disposal of the Ottoman Empire's territorial possessions in the Arab Levant -- an arrangement known as the Sykes-Picot Agreement -- provided the foundation for several years of struggle over the boundary between Palestine and Lebanon.[1] The agreement stated in part that Ottoman territories along the eastern shore of the Mediterranean would be divided into three zones: an "International Sphere" to be governed as an Allied condominium; a "British Sphere" encompassing the coastal towns of Haifa and Acre; and a "French Sphere" consisting of the coastal region north of the "International Sphere." This provisional partition is depicted on Figure 1.1.[2] It is worth noting that the line between the French and International Spheres ran from the coast through Lake Tiberias. The significance of this -- which apparently did not occur to the principals at the time -- was that it divided existing Jewish settlements between the two jurisdictions.

It was not until over two years later that Great Britain and France were obliged to translate the map drawings of 1916 into actual zones of military occupation. During those two years some critical events had taken place. Whereas in 1916 Grey had been forced to take into account the fact that France was carrying the greatest burden in the war against the Central Powers, by 1918 the fight against the Turks in the Levant had become a predominantly British affair. Furthermore, as manifested by the Balfour Declaration of 2 November 1917, Great Britain had formalized an alliance with the politically influential Zionist movement, personified by Dr. Chaim Weizmann. Thus, when it came time to create occupation zones, new lines were drawn to reflect new realities. On 19 September 1918 the Allies established Occupied Enemy Territorial Administrations (O.E.T.A.) in order to provide military government for conquered Ottoman jurisdictions in the eastern Mediterranean coastal region.[3]

Figure 1.2 shows the O.E.T.A. boundary.[4] It will be noted that the "Inter-national Sphere" no longer existed. In its place

3

FIGURE 1.1: ORIGINAL "SYKES-PICOT"
BOUNDARIES, MAY 1916

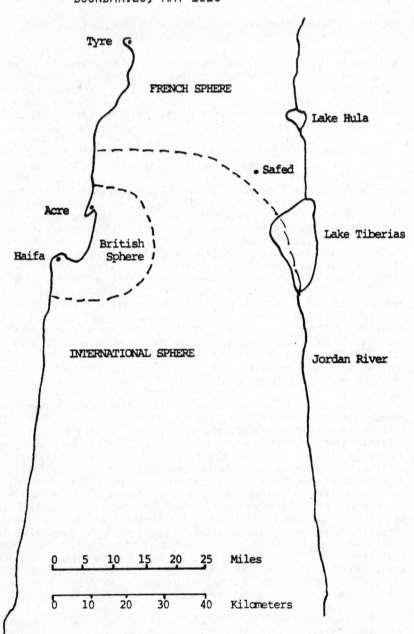

FIGURE 1.2: REVISED "O.E.T.A." BOUNDARY, AUTUMN 1918

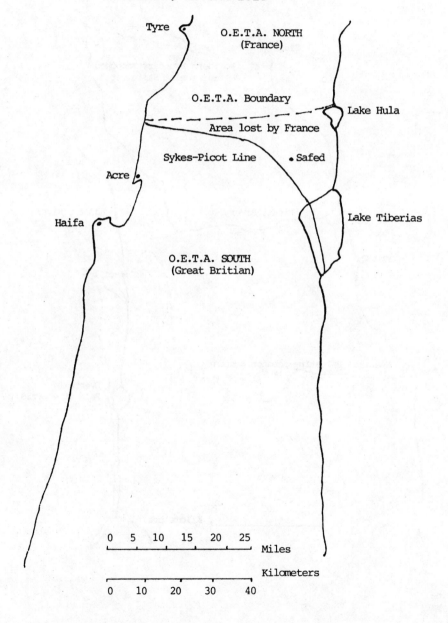

Tyre

O.E.T.A. NORTH
(France)

O.E.T.A. Boundary

Lake Hula

Area lost by France

Sykes-Picot Line

• Safed

Acre

Lake Tiberias

Haifa

O.E.T.A. SOUTH
(Great Britian)

0 5 10 15 20 25
Miles

Kilometers

0 10 20 30 40

FIGURE 1.3: THE "OFFICIAL" ZIONIST BOUNDARY PROPOSAL

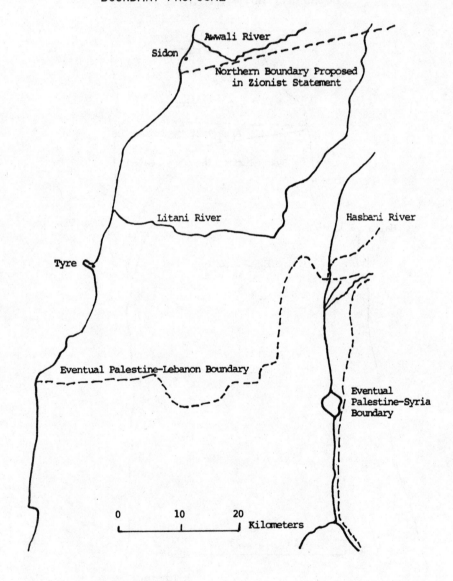

was "O.E.T.A South," an exclusively British zone of occupation. Furthermore, the boundary itself was moved north by the British in order to incorporate within O.E.T.A. South the Jewish settlements in the Safed area. These unilateral actions, reflecting as they did the preponderance of British arms in the region, were grudgingly accepted by France. In December 1918 Premier Georges Clemenceau of France agreed that "Palestine" -- defined for the moment as O.E.T.A. South -- would be exclusively British. The seizure of the Safed subdistrict by the British commander, General Allenby, was acknowledged with some bitterness by the French, who subsequently stubbornly resisted further boundary concessions.[5] Ironically, the new O.E.T.A. line still left some Jewish settlements within O.E.T.A. North, the French zone of occupation.

In 1918 "Palestine" still did not exist as a political entity. Although Djemal Pasha, the Ottoman wartime governor of Syria, held that "Palestine" as a geographical expression included the Ottoman districts of Jerusalem, Nablus, and Acre, there was simply no jurisdiction so named.[6] Great Britain intended, however, to create one. The problem of transforming zones of military occupation into internationally recognized protectorates required definitive agreements between Great Britain and France.

Notwithstanding Clemenceau's concession of "Palestine" to Great Britain,[7] the matter of where Palestine ended and where the French zone began was still very much a matter for negotiation. Great Britain's interest in Palestine's northern boundary can best be described as sentimentally ill-defined. The British had succeeded in getting Palestine for themselves through a combination of military superiority and Zionist political support, and in so doing they had thwarted direct French access to the Sinai Peninsula and Suez Canal. That Palestine's northern limit should be on the Litani River, or Lake Hula, or any of a dozen or more other places was of little importance to the British Empire. It was, of course, a matter of urgent importance to the Zionist allies of Great Britain, who were interested in procuring for Palestine a defensible boundary and one which would include within Palestine the abundant water resources of Upper Galilee. The French, eased out of the Sykes-Picot "International Sphere" and angry with British high-handedness in the drawing of the O.E.T.A. line, simply wanted to concede nothing more to Great Britain. Finding himself caught between specific Zionist boundary demands and French intransigence, British Prime Minister David Lloyd George adopted as his boundary policy a Biblical slogan which held that Palestine should extend "From Dan to Beersheba."[8]

At a time when prime ministers of Israel have justified their settlements policy in the Occupied Territories in part by referring to God's boundaries for "Eretz Israel" (the Land of Israel), it seems ironic that in the years immediately following World War I the Zionist leaders wanted nothing to do with Lloyd George's Biblical diplomacy. While British Protestant statesmen were thumping tables in favor of "Dan to Beersheba," the Zionists were writing thoughtful boundary proposals based on security and

8

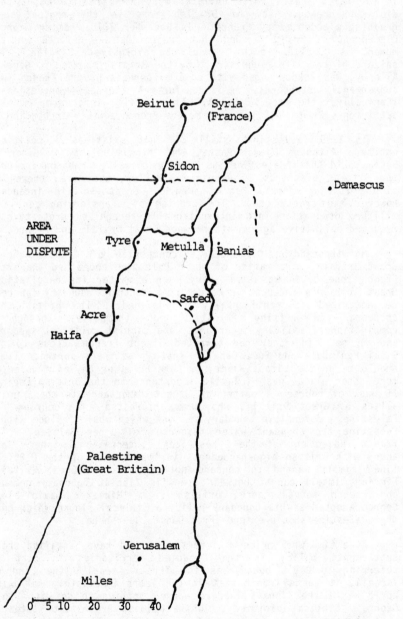

FIGURE 1.4: DISPUTED AREA,
MARCH - SEPTEMBER 1919

economic considerations for what they hoped would someday be a
Jewish State. On 27 February 1919 the Zionist Organization placed
before the Supreme Council at the Paris Peace Conference a
boundary proposal dated 3 February 1919.[9] In deference to France's
status as an ally of Great Britain, the Zionist Organization
refrained from using security arguments in support of its boundary
proposal. The main justification for the boundary request was the
inclusion within Palestine of the Litani River and the headwaters
of Mount Hermon.   The proposed line, which ran from the
Mediterranean coast south of Saida, northeast across the Litani
River, and eventually turned south toward the Golan Heights, is
depicted on Figure 1.3.[10]

On 17 March 1919 France rejected the Zionist claim.
Clemenceau handed Lloyd George a note stating that France would
insist upon the original Sykes-Picot line.[11] Thus, the two extreme
territorial claims, depicted on Figure 1.4, were established.

Just as the British had used the Zionists to advance their
interests in the Levant, so the French used Lebanese Christian
nationalists as a counterweight. In August 1919 France sponsored
a Lebanese delegation headed by the Maronite Patriarch,
Monseigneur Huwayyik, at the Paris Peace Conference. On 27 August
Huwayyik presented a memorandum of his own, which demanded that
Lebanon be detached from a larger "Syrian" entity; that Lebanon,
for economic reasons, be made as large as possible; and that
France be granted a mandate over the Lebanese State.[12]

There was no further movement until September 1919 when Great
Britain put forward a compromise known as the "Deauville
Proposal." In an Aide-Memoire dated 13 September and handed to
the French, Great Britain -- which still had forces in Beirut --
affirmed its intention to withdraw all of its forces from areas
promised to France in previous agreements. Point six stated that
"The territories occupied by British troops will then be
Palestine, defined in accordance with its ancient boundaries of
Dan to Beersheba ..."[13] As shown on Figure 1.5, the Deauville
Proposal called for a boundary following the Qasimiyya (Litani)
River from the coast, and then continuing eastward encompassing
the village of Banias, thought (incorrectly) by British statesmen
to be the ancient Dan. By virtue of this proposal Great Britain
formally commited itself in writing to the Dan to Beersheba
formula. It was this commitment, founded on the slippery basis of
Scriptural geography, that ultimately undermined the Zionist
effort to include all or part of the lower Litani River within
Palestine.

In February 1920 France sealed the fate of the Deauville
Proposal by specifically insisting that the Litani River remain
entirely within Lebanon.   Seeing that the French negotiator,
Foreign Minister Philippe Berthelot, would not give in with regard
to the Litani, Lloyd George took the final step which totally
undermined the Zionist position.

10

FIGURE 1.5: THE "DEAUVILLE LINE,"
SEPTEMBER 1919

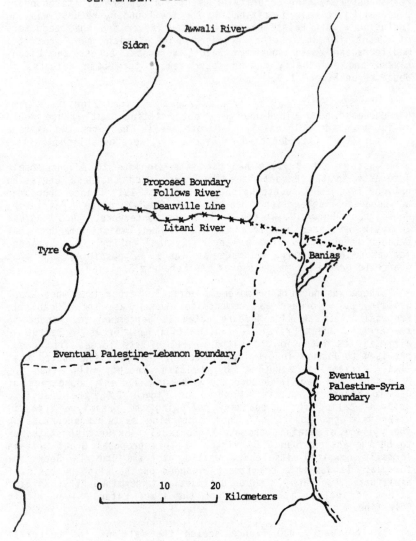

Mr. Lloyd George said he would like to recognize the
very conciliatory and helpful spirit in which M.
Berthelot had approached the subject, and he begged to
assure him that the British Government would respond in a
like spirit. These questions were to be settled as
between Allies and friends, and not as between
competitors. However, he thought the present conference
was not one in which details of frontiers could be
determined. A book written by a Scottish theological
professor, Professor Adam Smith, had been brought to his
notice. The book had been written before the war, and
although the work of a theologian, was so accurate in
matters of geography that it had been used by Lord
Allenby during his campaign.[14]

Lloyd George had known for quite some time what Smith's book
contained, because several months earlier, when preparing the
Deauville Proposal, he had ordered Professor Smith's book and
Atlas of the Historical Geography of the Holy Land be sent to him
in Paris.[15] Plate 34 of the Atlas, depicting "Palestine Under
David and Solomon," was the map used by Lloyd George to form his
own conception of Palestine's territorial extent. Figure 1.6 is
an approximation of the key map in Smith's Atlas, a map which
Berthelot no doubt examined with great interest. It can be seen
that although Samaria did touch the Litani in the northeast, it
did not even reach Acco (Acre) in the northwest. Since the
western portion of the Sykes-Picot line had already been drawn
north of Acre, it was reasonable to expect that the Palestine-
Lebanon boundary would be lowered somewhat in relation to the
Biblical standard in the east. This would leave the Litani
entirely outside of Palestine.

In June 1920 France proposed a compromise. It called
essentially for a line that would leave the coast at Ra's an
Naqurah, a few miles north of the Sykes-Picot/O.E.T.A. line, and
proceed eastward. It was then to turn sharply north, so as to
include within Palestine a "finger" of territory containing the
northernmost Jewish settlement (Metulla) and the Hula Valley.[16]
The inclusion of this "finger" was a direct consequence of the Tel
Hai massacre, which had taken place just three months earlier.
The Litani was left completely under French control.

With the northern settlements safely within Palestine, the
Zionists then waged a determined rearguard action from June
through December 1920 aimed at salvaging the Litani River. The
following exerpt of a letter from Dr. Weizmann to Lord Curzon,
dated 30 October 1920, clearly reflects both the determination and
exasperation of the Zionists.

Your Lordship, I am sure, realises the enormous
importance of the Litany to Palestine. Even if the whole
of the Jordan and the Yarmuk are included in Palestine,
it has insufficient water for its needs. The summer in
Palestine is extremely dry, and evaporation rapid and

12

FIGURE 1.6: PLATE 34, SMITH'S <u>ATLAS</u>

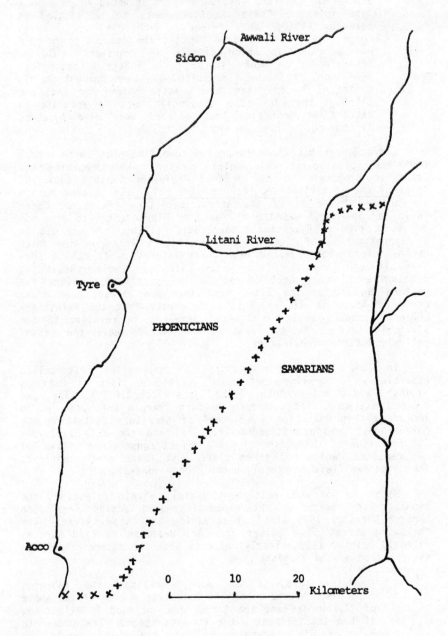

intense. The irrigation of Upper Galilee and the power
necessary for even a limited industrial life must come
from the Litany.   Experts agree that the Litany is of
little use to the well-watered Lebanon and we have always
agreed that the requirements of the territory not
included in Palestine should be adequately met.

It is hardly possible that France even realises the
extent to which the frontier she has proposed would
cripple the economic life of Palestine. For if Palestine
were cut off from the Litany, Upper Jordan and Yarmuk, to
say nothing of the western shore of the Galilee, she
could not be economically independent. <u>And a poor and
impoverished Palestine would be of no advantage to any
Power</u>. (Emphasis added.)[17]

Weizmann's appeal to British imperial sentiments was useless. In
his autobiography he stated that, "I tried to convince General
Gouraud the French High Commissioner in Beirut of the importance
to Palestine of the waters of the river Litani, but could arouse
no interest."[18]

Although middle level British negotiators charged with
transforming the Lloyd George-Berthelot understanding into a
treaty tried their very best to satisfy the Zionists, they found
themselves thoroughly undermined by the Prime Minister's Biblical
diplomacy. Part of a letter written by one of the British
diplomats illustrates this point.

As our case for extended Palestine frontiers had always
been argued at the Supreme Council generally on the
'historical' ground and in particular (however
unfortunate it may now seem) on the basis of plate No. 34
of Adam Smith's <u>Atlas of the Historical Geography of the
Holy Land</u>, you will readily understand how difficult it
was to meet the French argument as regards the inclusion
in Palestine of territory east of the Jordan and north of
the Yarmuk. It would not have been so difficult, if the
above plate be taken as the test, to argue for a frontier
including part of the Litani but, as I have said, the
course of the discussion at San Remo practically excluded
that point being taken up again.[19]

Final agreement in principle was reached by Great Britain and
France on 23 December 1920. The French proposal of the previous
June was accepted entirely with regard to the Palestine-Lebanon
boundary. A commission was established to demarcate the exact
line of the boundary, and on the subject of water, Article 8 of
the Franco-British Convention provided that

Experts nominated respectively by the administrations of
Syria and Palestine shall examine in common within six
months after the signature of the present convention the
employment, for the purposes of irrigation and the

production of hydroelectric power, of the waters of the
Upper Jordan and the Yarmuk and of their tributaries,
after satisfaction of the needs of the territories under
the French mandate.

In connection with this examination the French government
will give its representatives the most liberal
instructions for the employment of the surplus of these
waters for the benefit of Palestine.[20]

It should be noted that the Franco-British Convention made no
mention whatsoever of the Litani River.

The boundary commission established by the Franco-British
Convention submitted its final report in February 1922.[21] "This
agreement was signed on the 3rd February 1922. It was ratified by
the British Government on the 7th March 1923, and came into effect
three days later."[22]

The final agreement made no further mention of Zionist access
to French-controlled waters. The only aspect of the boundary left
subject to possible renegotiation was a short stretch of border
between Metulla and Banias, half of which was part of the
Palestine-Lebanon boundary and half of which divided Palestine and
Syria. The boundary had been drawn parallel to and 100 meters
south of a path linking Metulla and Banias. France had insisted
on keeping the entire path so as to preserve and control an east-
west road link. The final agreement upheld the French position
but included a provision stating that

The British Government shall be free to reopen the
question of readjusting the frontier between Banias and
Metallah on such terms as may be agreed between the two
mandatory Powers with a view of making the north road
between these two villages the final frontier.[23]

NOTES

1. The text of the Sykes-Picot Agreement may be found in E. L.
Woodward and Rohan Butler, ed., Documents on British Foreign
Policy 1919-1939. First Series Volume IV 1919 (London: His
Majesty's Stationery Office, 1952), pp. 241-251. Subsequent
references to these edited diplomatic documents will appear under
the citation of Documents, with the series and volume numbers.

2. Figure 1.1 is drawn from two sources: H.F. Frischwasser-
Ra'anan, The Frontiers of a Nation (London: The Batchworth Press,
1955), p. 151; and Jukka Nevakivi, Britain, France and the Arab
Middle East 1914-1920 (London: The Athlone Press, 1969), p.38.

3. Stephen Hemsley Longrigg, _Syria and Lebanon Under French Mandate_ (London: Oxford University Press, 1958), p. 66.

4. Figure 1.2 is based on Frischwasser-Ra'anan, _The Frontiers of a Nation_, p. 153.

5. "Ignorant deliberement la limite Sykes-Picot, le general Allenby avait, des Octobre 1918, deplace la frontiere vers le nord en rattachant le caza de Safed a la zone palestinienne. Jugeant cette acquisition encore insuffisante, les Brittaniques pretendaient englober dans la Palestine le cours presque entier du Jourdain, celui du Yarmuk, et le cours inferieur du Litani... Jean Pichon, _Le Partage du Proche Orient_ (Paris: J. Peyronnet & Cie, 1938), p. 188.

6. Cemal Pasa, _Memories of a Turkish Statesman_ (London: Hutchinson & Co., 1922), p. 154.

7. Clemenceau's acquiescence, along with his cession of Mosul to British Iraq, constituted the so-called "Clemenceau-Lloyd George agreement." See David Lloyd George, _The Truth About the Peace Treaties_ (London: Victor Gollancz Ltd, 1938), Volume 2, p. 1038.

8. "Now, as regards the future of Palestine... I imagine we shall agree that we must recover for Palestine its old boundaries. The old phrase 'Dan to Beersheba' still prevails. Whatever the administrative sub-divisions, we must recover for Palestine, be it Hebrew or Arab, the boundaries up to the Litani on the coast, and across to Banias, the old Dan, or Huleh in the interior." Lord Curzon, as cited by Doreen Ingrams, _Palestine Papers 1917-1922: Seeds of Conflict_ (London: John Murray, 1972), p. 49.

9. _Statement of the Zionist Organization Regarding Palestine_, 3 February 1919, 14 pp. Copy available at Hoover Library, Stanford University.

10. Figure 1.5 is based on the text of the _Statement of the Zionist Organization Regarding Palestine_, and on an explanation of the Zionist claim found in Frischwasser-Ra'anan, _The Frontiers of a Nation_, p. 107.

11. Pichon, _Le Partage du Proche Orient_, pp. 188-189.

12. Zeine N. Zeine, _The Struggle for Arab Independence_ (Beirut: Khayat's, 1960), p. 122.

13. The complete text of the _Aide-Memoire_ may be found in _Documents_, First Series Volume I, pp. 700-701.

14. _Documents_, First Series Volume VII, p. 115.

15. Ingrams, _Palestine Papers_, p. 76.

16. Frischwasser-Ra'anan, _The Frontiers of a Nation_, p. 136.

17. _Documents_, First Series Volume XIII, p. 419.

18. Chaim Weizmann, _Trial and Error_ (New York: Harper & Brothers, 1949), p. 289.

19. _Documents_, First Series Volume XIII, p. 419.

20. _Franco-British Convention of December 23, 1920, on Certain Points Connected with the Mandates for Syria and the Lebanon, Palestine and Mesopotamia_, Cmd. 1195. (London: His Majesty's Stationery Office, 1921), p. 4.

21. _Agreement Between His Majesty's Government and the French Government Respecting the Boundary Line Between Syria and Palestine from the Mediterranean to El Hamme_, Cmd. 1910. (London: His Majesty's Stationery Office, 1923).

22. H. W. V. Temperley, ed., _A History of the Peace Conference at Paris_, Volume VI (London: Henry Frowde and Hodder & Stoughton, 1924), p. 166.

23. _Agreement Between His Majesty's Government and the French Government_, Cmd. 1910., pp. 5-8.

2. Local Implications
of the 1923 Boundary Agreement

The Palestine-Lebanon boundary agreed upon in 1923 bisected three natural geographical regions: the Galilean Coast, Upper Galilee, and that portion of the Great Rift Valley lying to the east of Upper Galilee. Figure 2.1 is an approximation of the three regions in question.[1]

It is not likely that the British and French diplomats who partitioned Upper Galilee and the adjoining regions imagined the impact their action would have on the inhabitants of the area. Had they known, it is even less likely that they would have cared. The area was an economic and social backwater, a depressed region populated almost entirely by Arabs (except of course for those few Jewish settlements around the Hula Valley) engaged in subsistence agriculture. It hardly seemed possible that the drawing of an international boundary through such an area would have much of an impact, positive or negative, on anything.

Yet for the Arab inhabitants of the new frontier region the boundary was at best an inconvenience and at worst a potential economic and security disaster. Its very demarcation--a seemingly innocuous piece of surveying--caused unwelcomed changes. Prior to the boundary imposition the Marj and Hula Valleys had functioned as an economic unit. According to Karmon the village of Marj 'Uyun served as the area's urban center. "Here lived the landowners, the proprietors of the water mills, the grain merchants and moneylenders, on whom the inhabitants of the Hula Valley depended. With the establishment of the British mandate, Marj 'Uyun became part of Lebanon."[2] The boundary partitioned the region and left the Hula Valley without an urban center until the creation of Qiryat Shemona by Israel.[3] Although Hourani maintains that "There was no good reason, economic or ethnic, for the inclusion of the Hulah district in Palestine,"[4] it is probably more accurate to conclude that it was the regional partition itself--irrespective of which side gained or lost--that made little sense. Had it not been for the existence of a few vulnerable Jewish settlements, it is likely that the Hula and Marj Valleys would have remained united under the French jurisdiction.

Upper Galilee also suffered from the demarcation. Traditionally the village of Bint Jubayl, which ended up in Lebanon, had served as an important junction for roads leading to Tyre from Acre, Safed, and the Hula Valley.[5] Although the coastal road would eventually have become the primary land link between Acre and Tyre, it is nevertheless true that Bint Jubayl's role in Upper Galilee was seriously jeopardized by the appearance of a boundary. Much the same can be said for the Palestinian town of Safed, which would probably have emerged as the principal urban

FIGURE 2.1: GEOGRAPHICAL REGIONS

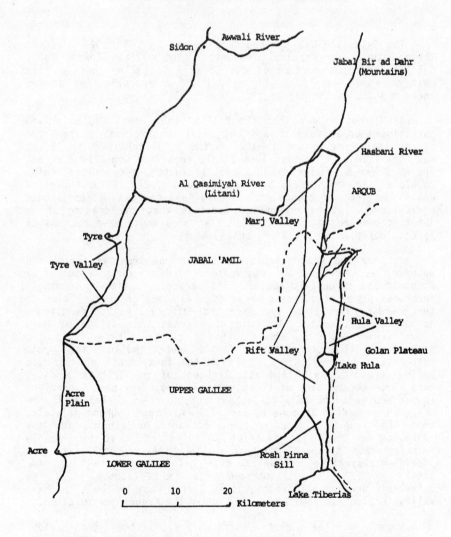

center for all of Upper Galilee.[6]   Regrettably, however, the
boundary nullified the area's few potentialities and worsened an
already bleak economic picture.

Yet that was not all. If the mere act of drawing a boundary
caused disruptions, its eventual closure could lead to
catastrophe. One of the few things that mitigated the poverty of
the area was the ability of people to move freely to graze
livestock, sell produce, and seek odd jobs for cash. The presence
of an international boundary threatened to change that.   If
political problems were ever to cause the border to close, the
economic options of the Arab farmers and villagers on both sides
of the line would be reduced. They would be obliged either to
accept an even lower standard of living, or else flock to the
cities of their respective countries in order to find employment.
The citizens of southern Lebanon were particularly vulnerable to
the potential effects of a border closing due to their own central
government's lack of interest in developing the economy of the
area.

Soon after the boundary demarcation went into effect in 1924,
the mandatory authorities in Jerusalem and Beirut discovered that
the inhabitants of the frontier area were acting as if no border
existed. Rather than attempting to physically block human traffic
from moving across the border--a policy which probably would have
prompted violent resistance--the British and French officials
wisely chose instead to legalize the border crossing habits of
their subjects. On 2 February 1926 an agreement was signed
involving Palestine, Lebanon, and Syria. The accord aimed at
"regulating certain administrative matters in connection with the
frontier" in such a way as to facilitate "good neighbourly
relations in connection with frontier questions." The treaty
defined the frontier region as including the subdistricts of Acre
and Safed in Palestine; Tyre, Marj 'Uyun, and Hasbaya in Lebanon;
and Quneitra in Syria.[7]

The agreement constituted an attempt to deal with problems
caused by the boundary demarcation. One such problem was the
status of private, village, and religious property which had been
bisected by the boundary. Instead of asking for a new
demarcation, the 1926 accord left the boundary as it was and
established equitable procedures governing the collection of taxes
on divided property and subsequent title transfers.[8] The accord
also stated that grazing, cultivation, and water rights predating
the boundary would remain in effect. The following passage
specified the border-crossing rights of the local inhabitants:

> They shall be entitled...to cross the frontier freely and
> without a passport and to transport, from one side to the
> other of the frontier, their animals and the natural
> increase thereof, their tools, their vehicles, their
> implements, seeds and products of the soil or subsoil of
> their lands, without paying any customs duties or any
> dues for grazing or watering or any other tax on account

of passing the frontier and entering the neighbouring territory.[9]

Another provision of the accord permitted the people of the frontier area to transport (duty free) across the boundary any crops or local industrial goods produced anywhere within the frontier zone destined for family consumption in any of the subdistricts covered by the agreement.[10]

The treaty also facilitated the maintenance of public order along the common border. Police from both sides were permitted to use tracks and roads which ran along parts of the boundary "without passport or toll of any kind."[11] Furthermore, Palestinian police and civilians were granted the use, for their convenience, of certain paths located wholly within Lebanon.[12] In cases of emergency the signatories were allowed "to use the tracks and roads forming the frontier for any movement of troops, but notice of such use shall be given to the other Government concerned as soon as possible."[13] However, neither side was granted the right of "hot pursuit" in attempts to apprehend common criminals, political dissidents, or marauders seeking refuge on the other side of the border.[14]

The "good neighbourly relations" accord of 1926 enabled the people of the frontier region to escape--though only temporarily-- the greatest dangers inherent in the creation of the boundary. The benefits of the liberal frontier policy accrued most noticeably to the citizens of southern Lebanon. Thanks to Beirut's lack of interest, the region functioned economically for several years as a virtual extension of northern Palestine. According to one observer,

> During the Mandatory period most South Lebanese families had at least one member working in Palestine; and a large number of frontier villages lived on the proceeds of smuggling--hashish (en route to Egypt), arms and food-stuffs, and often "illegal" Jewish immigrants to Palestine; Jewish manufactured goods to Lebanon and Syria.[15]

The Arab-Israeli war of 1948 and the subsequent General Armistice Agreement between Israel and Lebanon caused the suspension of the 1926 agreement. The treaty was completely voided on 30 October 1953, when Israel's ambassador to the United Nations announced that "Israel does not inherit the international treaties signed by the United Kingdom as mandatory power."[16] The closing of the border was a severe blow to southern Lebanon, as the 1948 war caused a dramatic demographic transformation in the frontier region. On Israel's side of the line Arab villages were vacated during and after the fighting, and occupied by Jewish settlers who had neither the need nor inclination to develop economic relationships with their Arab neighbors on Lebanon's side of the border. Cut off from economic opportunities in Israel, southern Lebanon languished. Beirut's traditional lack of concern for the predominantly Shi'a region was reinforced by the belief, commonly held by members of Lebanon's political elite, that Israel would someday seize the area anyway. By the latter part of the 1960s the south's misery was compounded by fighting in the frontier area between Palestinian commandos and the Israel Defense Force. Again Beirut seemed justified in not investing significantly in southern Lebanon. Yet, as The Economist pointed out,

> The presence of the Palestinian guerrilla units and the Israeli raids have provided an excuse for inaction, but it is hard not to suspect there has been a lack of concern for the section of the population which is least strongly represented in the corridors of power.[17]

The great suffering endured by the people of southern Lebanon, consisting of economic depression compounded in recent years by widespread death and destruction, is undoubtedly the most lamentable consequence of the 1920 Franco-British Convention.

NOTES

1. Figure 2.1 is based on information contained in Efraim Orni and Elisha Efrat, Geography of Israel (Philadelphia: The Jewish Publication Society of America, 1971).

2. Yehuda Karmon, "The Drainage of the Huleh Swamps," Geographical Review, April 1960, p. 191.

3. Ibid., p. 192.

4. A. H. Hourani, Syria and Lebanon: A Political Essay (London: Oxford University Press, 1946), p. 56.

5. Yehuda Karmon, Israel: A Regional Geography (London: Wiley Interscience, 1971), p. 73.

6. Ibid.

7. Agreement Between Palestine and Syria and the Lebanon to Facilitate Good Neighbourly Relations in Connection with Frontier Questions (London: His Majesty's Stationery Office, 1927), pp. 1, 8.

8. Ibid., pp. 4, 6.

9. Ibid., p. 4.

10. Ibid., p. 8.

11. Ibid., p. 2.

12. Ibid.

13. Ibid., p. 4.

14. Ibid., p. 6.

15. Ray Alan, "Lebanon: Israel's Friendliest Neighbor," Commentary, Volume 13 Number 6, June 1952, p. 556.

16. Abraham H. Hirsh, "Utilization of International Rivers in the Middle East," American Journal of International Law, Volume 50, Number 1, January 1956, p. 81n. According to Kenneth J. Keith, Israel is the only state which refuses to "succeed" to the treaties made by its predecessor. See "Succession to Bilateral Treaties by Seceding States," American Journal of International Law, Volume 61 Number 2, April 1967, p. 524.

17. "Not Just a Tiny Strip of Land," The Economist, 26 January 1974, p. 15 of a special insert survey on Lebanon.

3. National and International Implications of the 1923 Boundary Agreement

The impact of the new boundary was not limited to the inhabitants of the frontier region. The decision of Great Britain and France to place the boundary where they did carried with it some significant implications for both Zionism and Christian Lebanese nationalism.

From the Zionist perspective the implications of Palestine's new frontier were quite serious indeed. As Howard M. Sachar has observed,

> To the north and northeast, the country was deprived of almost all the major water resources--the Litani River, the northernmost sources of the Jordan, the spring of Hermon, and the greater part of the Yarmuk--needed for the power and irrigation plans that were even then being formulated... Moreover, by failing to approximate any natural geographic boundaries, the borders left the country all but indefensible militarily.[1]

Zionist misgivings about the new boundary were not, however, shared by Great Britain. The actual British approach to the question of water resources--as opposed to the negotiating posture maintained through the early months of 1920--may be summarized by the following exchange between some very prominent British officials which took place on 10 September 1919. Arthur Bonar Law, the Lord Privy Seal, asked his colleagues to define "the value of Palestine." General Allenby replied "that it had no economic value whatsoever." Lloyd George had nothing to say about economics but insisted nonetheless that "The mandate over Palestine would give us great prestige."[2] Later, when questioned in Parliament about his government's failure to secure the waters of the Litani River for Palestine, the Prime Minister responded by shouting,

> No! They have never been included in Palestine. The agreement entered into by M. Clemenceau and myself in December 1918 was that Palestine was to be old historic Palestine, that is, from Dan to Beersheba. That does not include the Litani River.[3]

The economy of Palestine was obviously not considered to be an issue of great importance to the British Empire.

Likewise Great Britain did not share the Zionist apprehension over the military aspects of the northern frontier. Having excluded France from playing a role in the governing of Palestine, the British had succeeded in placing strategic depth between the Suez Canal and French forces in the Levant. A northern defense line anchored on the Litani River, one which certainly would have appealed to the Zionists, would have added little to Britain's ability to defend the canal. Nevertheless, as Palestine's High Commissioner reported in 1925, "Palestine is a small territory, but it is broken up by hills and mountains... Its frontiers to the north and east are open at almost any point."[4] Indeed, one would be hard pressed to identify terrain anywhere along the boundary that is well suited for either defensive military operations or routine border security. This is especially true when the ground is viewed from the perspective of Palestine (Israel). After leaving the imposing natural obstacle of Ras an Naqurah, the boundary meanders along the open terrain of Upper Galilee, through wadis and along a plateau which slopes sharply to the south (into Israel) and gently toward the north (into Lebanon). Only along the Neftali Ridge, which overlooks the Hula Valley to the east and Wadi Ad Dubbah to the west, can terrain be identified as suitable (from the Israeli perspective) for security operations. The only "natural" feature of the area which tended to discourage attacks from the north was the fact that the major lines of communication in the Upper Galilee region ran west and east rather than north and south. Yet the Zionists of 1923, perhaps anticipating the day when force would help transform Palestine into a Jewish State, still had good reason to be dissatisfied with the security aspect of the northern boundary.

Notwithstanding the existence of substantial economic and security problems the Zionist movement was not, in 1923, in any position to reverse the Anglo-French decision on the northern frontier. It is clear, however, that the Zionists did retain hope that the boundary could someday be adjusted in Palestine's favor, and that such an adjustment need not come as a result of war. In the 1920s the French authorities in Beirut were approached on the subject of permitting Zionist settlements to be established in southern Lebanon. Dr. Weizmann himself reported that he was told by the French High Commissioner, "Of course... I would not want you to work in southern Syria, because immediately after you'd come to Tyre and Saida you would want the frontier rectified." Weizmann neither confirmed nor refuted the High Commissioner's observation.[5] It is in any event clear that although the northern boundary settlement frustrated Zionist economic and security planning, it did not shut the door on the matter forever. Instead of acknowledging their defeat and writing it off as a lesson learned in the tangled web of international diplomacy, Zionist leaders in Palestine continued to believe that their setback could somehow be reversed. As recently as 21 March 1978, the Defense Minister of Israel was berated by a member of the Knesset for not simply seizing the Litani River during that month's invasion of southern Lebanon. The MK, Mrs. Cohen, shouted, "Your uncle, the late President Weizman, knew at the time the historic significance of the Litani." Ezer Weizman's reply: "It is not from you that I will receive references about Hayyim Weizman."[6] In retrospect it appears that Dr. Chaim Weizmann's calm diplomacy, based as it was upon economic justifications for the inclusion of the Litani in Palestine, helped to insure that mainstream Zionist irredentism toward southern Lebanon would not have a strong religious

component. Unlike post-1948 Arab Jerusalem or that part of
Mandatory Palestine annexed by Jordan (the "West Bank"), few
Zionists would point to southern Lebanon as being part of the
"Eretz Israel" promised by God to the Hebrews. Had Weizmann
adopted some of Lloyd George's religious fervor and declared the
Litani to be part of Eretz Israel, Zionist irredentism probably
would have been fulfilled long ago.

Zionism's strong desire to expand Palestine in such a way as
to secure hydrographic resources and defensible terrain contrasted
sharply with the indifference shown by Christian Lebanese
nationalists toward their southern districts. France, to be sure,
had scored a "victory" by securing a very generous southern
frontier for the new state of Greater Lebanon. The new borders of
the Lebanese state substantially satisfied the expansionist dreams
of Christian Lebanese nationalists and served French imperial
interests by extending the political sway of a narrow, largely
Francophile Christian majority over the largest land area
possible. Yet by attaching the largely Shi'ite Muslim south[7] and
other Muslim areas to the predominantly Maronite Mount Lebanon,
France also institutionalized unrest within the Lebanese political
system. Philip Hitti pointed out that the creation of Greater
Lebanon by France was at best a mixed blessing and at worst a
political time bomb. "What the country gained in area it lost in
cohesion. It lost its internal equilibrium, though geographically
and economically it became more viable. The Christian
overwhelming majority was seriously reduced."[8]

To understand the attitude of Greater Lebanon's political
elite toward the south, one must recall that the "Lebanese
nationalism" of the late nineteenth and early twentieth centuries
was really an outgrowth of the Maronite national identity which
had developed during that sect's 1,000-year occupation of Mount
Lebanon. Inasmuch as Greater Lebanon was the offspring of
Christian Lebanese nationalism and French imperialism, it comes as
no great surprise that the rulers of the new political entity
manifested little interest in the rural, poor, and predominantly
non-Christian south. Consequently, "The French concentrated their
development efforts on the mountain and Beirut..."[9] By ignoring
the south France accurately reflected the desires of the Lebanese
political elite. Even after independence, the first President of
the Lebanese Republic, Bishara al-Khouri, reportedly asserted that
"the 'Lebaneseness' (Lubnaniyat) of the predominantly Shi'a
southern region had not been finally established," and for that
reason the area was not entitled to large-scale developmental
assistance.[10] Recent research has also revealed that in 1932
Emile Edde, a leading Maronite politician who would serve as his
country's President from 1936 to 1941, tried to convince France to
get rid of Lebanon's southern region. He wrote a memorandum to
the Under-Secretary of State in the French Foreign Ministry
suggesting (among other things) that southern Lebanon, consisting
as it did of an overwhelming Shi'a majority, be detached from
Lebanon and transformed into an autonomous state under a French
administrator.[11] Although France never acted upon Edde's

suggestion, the memorandum provides an insight into the thinking of a leading member of the Maronite elite during the mandate period and helps to explain why the Lebanese government paid little attention to the needs or potentialities of the south.

Beirut's policy of ignoring the south would eventually facilitate the destruction of Lebanon itself. The south, regarded by Lebanon's leaders as a virtually useless appendage, became a military vacuum which in some areas was eventually filled by Palestinian commandos, who would use it as a base from which to attack Israeli military and civilian targets. The absence of an effective official Lebanese presence in the frontier area encouraged Israel to act unilaterally against the armed Palestinians. Consequently Lebanon suffered repeated attacks at the hands of Israel, some of which were in retaliation for the activities of Palestinian commandos and terrorists, but all of which had the objective of forcing a confrontation in Lebanon between Christian Lebanese nationalists (who wanted nothing to do with the Arab-Israeli conflict) and Palestinian/pan-Arab nationalists, for whom the struggles against Zionism and the Maronite elite were regarded as virtually synonomous. By the spring of 1975 civil war began to consume Lebanon, a disaster which probably could have been avoided had the authorities in Beirut made sincere efforts from the beginning to build a state and integrate the south into the rest of the country. Yet southern Lebanon's "value" to the Christian Lebanese nationalists of the post-World-War-I era lay solely in the space it occupied on the map. The inclusion of the area in Greater Lebanon satisfied the emotional yearning of Lebanese nationalists for the territory of "historic" Lebanon, but the land and the people living on it were irrelevant to the political and economic processes taking place in Paris and Beirut.

The broad political significance of the 1923 boundary settlement can therefore be summarized as follows: Palestine was deprived of an area which the Zionists wanted and which they thought they needed very badly; Lebanon was handed a piece of territory which it "wanted," but for which it had no particular use; and the Arabs living in the contested region were considered to be irrelevant by everyone concerned. The Anglo-French compromise may have helped to facilitate a smooth working relationship between the two wartime allies, but the cost was high. Zionism lost an area which it deemed essential for the defense and development of Palestine; Lebanon gained an area which would later prove to be an enormous political liability; and the people of the frontier region found their livelihoods and eventually their lives in jeopardy. It was the fundamental assymetry between Zionist appreciation for southern Lebanon and Beirut's indifference toward the region that set the stage for disasters yet to come.

NOTES

1. Howard M. Sachar, The Emergence of the Middle East: 1914-24 (New York: Alfred A. Knopf, 1969), p. 284. It should also be noted, however, that in addition to including the northern Jewish settlements within Palestine, the British and Zionists secured from France two water-related concessions at the expense not of Lebanon, but of Syria. First, that part of the Jordan River north of Lake Tiberias was kept entirely within Palestine by demarcating the boundary about 500 meters to the east of the river. Second, Lake Tiberias itself was kept entirely within Palestine, including a ten meter-wide strip of its north-eastern shore. See Yehuda Karmon, Israel: A Regional Geography, p. 73.

2. Doreen Ingrams, Palestine papers 1917-1922: Seeds of Conflict (London: John Murray, 1972), p. 77.

3. Khalid Kishtainy, Whither Israel? A Study of Zionist Expansionism (Beirut: Palestine Liberation Organization Research Center, 1970), p. 21.

4. Herbert Samuel, Palestine. Report of the High Commissioner on the Administration of Palestine, 1920-1925 (London: His Majesty's Stationery Office, 1925), p. 3.

5. Chaim Weizmann, Trial and Error, the Autobiography of Chaim Weizmann (New York: Harper & Brothers, 1949), p. 366.

6. Jerusalem Domestic Service, 21 March 1978, as quoted by the Foreign Broadcast Information Service, FBIS-MEA-78-56, 22 March 1978, p. N3.

7. According to a census conducted by the French government in 1921, the sectarian composition of southern Lebanon's population was as follows: 13,397 Sunni Muslims (located mainly in the towns of Tyre and Sidon); 62,796 Shi'a Muslims; 3,519 Druze; and 31,071 Christians. See Arnold J. Toynbee, ed., Survey of International Affairs 1925 Volume I (London: Oxford University Press, 1927), p. 355.

8. Phillip K. Hitti. Lebanon in History: From the Earliest Times to the Present (New York: St. Martin's Press, 1967), p. 490.

9. "Not Just a Tiny Strip of Land," The Economist, 26 January 1974, p. 15 of a special insert survey onLebanon.

10. N. Raphaeli, "Development Planning: Lebanon," Western Political Quarterly, Volume XX No. 3, September 1967, p. 719.

11. Meir Zamir, "Emile Edde and the Territorial Integrity of Lebanon," Middle Eastern Studies, Volume 14, No. 2, May 1978, pp. 232-233.

4. The Evolving Water Controversy

During the six decades that elapsed between the 1923 Anglo-French boundary agreement and the 1983 Israel-Lebanon agreement, events in the frontier area alternately simmered and boiled over. Although the outside world took little note of this small, seemingly inconsequential area, it is nevertheless true that the frontier region saw very few years that were totally devoid of controversy and violence. Instead problems related to the Zionist objections to the boundary agreement -- namely, water and security -- continually manifested themselves in a variety of forms.

Between 1923 and 1968 the issue of southern Lebanon's abundant water resources and their disposition was the prime ingredient in the residue of distrust and disappointment left behind by the boundary settlement. The boundary agreements of 1920 and 1923 cut sharply into the most optimistic Zionist estimates of the amount of water available to support extensive Jewish agricultural colonization in Palestine. Zionist planners had hoped to divert part of the flow of the Litani River eastward into the Hasbani River, where it would flow south into the Jordan Valley and eventually be piped overland to the Negev Desert. Yet the 1920 compromise had left the Litani entirely within Lebanon, fewer than 4,000 tantalizing meters from the Palestine border. Furthermore, neither the 1920 nor the 1923 agreements even mentioned the Litani in the context of future bilateral development schemes. The 1920 accord, as noted above, did call for the creation of a commission to study the possibility of jointly exploiting the "Upper Jordan" (Hasbani) River. Yet as Hirsch commented in 1956, the commission "seems never to have been formed."[1] In short, the Zionists had failed to secure even limited access to the waters of southern Lebanon.

The issue of water resources in the Palestine/Israel-Lebanon frontier region will be examined in three aspects: (1) continuing Zionist interest in southern Lebanon's most important waterway, the Litani River; (2) the role played by independent Lebanon in Arab efforts to divert the headwaters of the Jordan River away from Israel's Hula Valley; and (3) the climax of water-related tensions before, during, and after the June 1967 Arab-Israeli war.

Zionism's "loss" of the Litani did not, at least during the mandatory period, translate into Lebanon's gain. Writing in 1936, Sa'id B. Himadeh commented that "At present the river is utilized to some extent for irrigation purposes but no use has yet been made of its generating powers."[2] The limited amount of irrigation undertaken by 1936 was restricted almost entirely to the fertile Biqa' and coastal plain,[3] and France's contribution to the river's exploitation (aside from plans and studies never effectuated) only amounted to a few flood-control projects completed between 1924 and 1928.[4] During World War II British military authorities in

Lebanon encouraged the "Qasimiyah Irrigation Scheme," which attempted to water the coastal plain "from Sidon to a point ten kilometers south of Tyre."[5] The plan was abandoned during the war but was later revived by independent Lebanon.

Franco-Lebanese neglect of the Litani did not go unnoticed by the Zionists. In 1934 the League of Nations gave its approval to the Anglo-French boundary agreement of 1923, "and after that the Zionist leaders slowly lost hope of ever achieving a change in the frontier line."[6] Yet in 1936 the Zionists received a small measure of encouragement in the matter of sharing with Lebanon the fruits of the Litani's presence in Upper Galilee. A study on regional electricity prepared for the American University of Beirut suggested that "The Litani concession in south Lebanon could advantageously be given to one company which would serve Sidon, Tyre, Nabatiyyah, the Marj 'Ayun district and possibly Safad in Palestine" Emphasis added .[7] In 1943 the Lebanese engineering firm of Alfred Naccache and Jewish engineers of the Palestine Water Cooperative conducted a joint study which concluded that Lebanon could usefully employ only one-seventh of the Litani's flow. The study recommended, therefore, that most of the water be diverted from a point near the river's "elbow" through a tunnel into Palestine. In return for the water, Lebanon would receive "all or part of the power produced by the drop from the mountains to the Jordan Valley." The study heartened the Zionists, whose "dreams of Negev development could not be fully realized without the Litani water."[8] It is worth noting, however,that the underlying assumption of the 1943 report was that Lebanon would use the Litani for irrigation only, and not for fully autonomous power production.

It certainly appeared, however, that the possibility of Zionist-Lebanese collaboration in the exploitation of the Litani was gaining momentum in the 1940s. Yet the Arab-Israeli war of 1948 served to fundamentally alter the prospects for such a cooperative undertaking. The Zionist victory had engendered much bitterness and recrimination in the Arab world, and the Lebanese government, built as it was upon the flimsy basis of local and confessional interests, could ill-afford to provoke Arab nationalists--both within and outside of Lebanon--by striking a quick bargain with the new Jewish State. Besides, as Charles Issawi pointed out, Lebanon "profited from the Arab-Israeli war and the subsequent boycott which eliminated the potential competition of the port of Haifa and the money market of Tel Aviv."[9] Furthermore, a study undertaken by the United Nations Economic Survey Mission for the Middle East in 1949 suggested that the projected hydroelectric needs of Lebanon were actually quite extensive, and that Lebanon could use far more of the Litani's flow than the meager fourteen percent envisioned by the survey of 1943. Yet the 1949 report left open the possibility that a portion of the Litani could be diverted over to the Hasbani for eventual use by Israel.[10]

Once the question of cooperative water development became wrapped up in the troubled politics of the area, Lebanese-Israeli collaboration became an impossibility. Any sign of Lebanese willingness to supply "Arab" water to the Negev, thereby facilitating Jewish immigration to Israel, would have been regarded as treachery not only by other Arab states, but by many Lebanese citizens as well. As Saliba has observed, "For Israel the development of its Negev area is not critically needed to feed the existing population. Rather the purpose is absorption of Jewish immigrants which Israel voluntarily seeks...for defensive purposes."[11]

Israel was not at all sympathetic with Lebanon's delicate position in the Arab world. During the course of fighting in 1948, Zionist forces had occupied a strip of Lebanese territory adjoining the "elbow" of the Litani River. Under the terms of the General Armistice Agreement signed in March 1949, Israeli units pulled back from the Litani and returned to what had been mandatory Palestine. According to Earl Berger, Israel's willingness to abandon its foothold on the Litani was predicated on its belief that Lebanon could be induced to sign a formal peace treaty. Thereafter, presumably, the two countries would have proceeded with the joint exploitation of the Litani envisioned by the 1943 report, and the infant Israeli state would at the same time avoid the international complications sure to follow any formal annexation of Lebanese territory. According to Berger, "If they the Israelis had felt...that the Lebanese did not also consider the negotiations as the penultimate step towards peace they would never have withdrawn."[12] Having failed to achieve through diplomacy that which its soldiers had won in combat, the Israeli leaders were once again forced to abandon plans of piping the abundant waters of the Litani southward to the Negev Desert.

In July 1953 Israel's cabinet approved a plan to draw water from the Jordan River at the Banat Ya'qub Bridge (north of Lake Tiberias) for diversion to the Negev. Although its failure to strike a bargain with Lebanon over the Litani had wrecked plans for large-scale desert irrigation, Israel decided that even a small Jewish agrarian presence in the Negev would be an important symbol of the vitality of the Jewish State. With or without Lebanese water, Israel was determined to make patches of the desert bloom.

Work on the canal, which would carry the water southward, began in September 1953. Due to international complications, however, the project was short-lived. The diversion point for the scheme was located in a demilitarized zone created by the 1949 Israeli-Syrian General Armistice Agreement. Syria protested that the project was a clear violation of that accord, and its position was supported both by United Nations observers and the United States. American opposition was underscored by the Eisenhower administration's decision to suspend all economic aid to Israel pending cessation of work on the project. Faced with a solid wall of international opposition, Israel stopped work on the diversion project on 27 October 1953.

The United States, which played the crucial role in forcing Israel to back down, believed that the potentially explosive water controversy could be converted into a showcase of Arab-Israeli cooperation. Regional cooperation over water, a substance needed by all regardless of political persuasion, could aid in the resettlement of Palestinian refugees and lead perhaps to political accomodations. America's decision to pursue peace in the Middle East by encouraging a multilateral water agreement served once again to focus attention on the Litani.

In October 1953 President Eisenhower dispatched a personal envoy, Mr. Eric Johnston, to the Middle East to try to convince Israel and the Arab states to undertake the joint development of the Jordan Valley. Johnston carried with him a plan drawn up in the offices of the engineering firm of Charles T. Main. The "Main Plan" called for a dam and reservoir to be built in Lebanon on the Hasbani River, but it excluded the Litani from the Arab-Israeli development plan "on the grounds that it is a Lebanese national river that could not be included in an international scheme."[13]

It was the Main Plan's omission of the Litani that prompted the loudest Israeli objections. To counter Johnston's proposal, Israel retained the services of John S. Cotton, an American engineer. The "Cotton Plan," unveiled in February 1954, constituted Israel's negotiating position with regard to water. It tied the Litani into a regional development scheme and estimated that the surplus water not needed for irrigation in Lebanon amounted to nearly fifty percent of the river's flow. Accordingly the Cotton Plan urged that large quantities of Litani water be diverted to Israel from a point near Marj 'Uyun. As one observer noted at the time of the negotiations,

> Given the right atmosphere...the Israelis hope Lebanon might be induced to give Israel Litani water in exchange for power. They hope Lebanon would on this basis sell up to 400,000,000 cubic meters per annum of the Litani's flow of about 850,000,000 cubic meters.[14]

As was the case with the 1943 report, Israel's hopes for access to the Litani rested on the assumption that Lebanon would not attempt to harness the river's hydroelectric potential on its own.

It must be emphasized that Israel's "hope" of Lebanese cooperation was simply that: a hope. As Brecher pointed out, "while a strong case could be made on technical and geo-economic grounds, Israel's legal claim was non-existent; the Litani was a wholly national river--of an enemy state."[15] James Hudson agreed, stating that "Since Israel has no real share of the Litani Basin, it has no claim by right under international law to any Litani water."[16] Therefore, according to Peretz, "Israel stood a far better chance of eventually obtaining some Litani water if an acceptable arrangement were first made and executed with the Arab states for the Jordan. Such an agreement might pave the way for a deal with Lebanon later on."[17] In the absence of such an agreement, an accord with Lebanon seemed out of the question. As James Hudson has pointed out,

> With the continuing Arab-Israel dispute, Lebanon would not risk its standing in the Arab world to sell water to Israel. Secondly, if an arrangement were made, past decades of suspicion might be difficult to overcome. Israel would possibly be unwilling to rely on Lebanese goodwill as a guarantee of future deliveries, and Lebanon would be hesitant to allow Israel an interest in Lebanese water that might give an excuse for intervention. Finally, if Lebanon did sell water out of the country, past the eyes of the Shi'a farmers in the south who do not have irrigation water, there would be considerable local discontent.[18]

Israel apparently recognized that it would be impossible for the politically fragmented Lebanese Republic to break ranks with the other Arab states and sign a water-sharing agreement. In early 1955 Israel dropped its claim to a share of the Litani's waters and even permitted the idea of a Hasbani River dam to die in negotiations.[19] It appeared at first that Israel's flexible bargaining position would lead to an agreement on the joint Arab-Israeli development of the Jordan Valley, and that such an accord would free Lebanon from the unspoken prohibition placed upon it against making a deal with Israel. During the summer of 1955 an Arab-Israeli water compromise seemed to be within reach. Yet on 11 October of the same year the Arab League decided against signing an agreement with the Jewish state.

Twice therefore, in 1949 and 1955, Israel withdrew from the Litani--once militarily and once diplomatically--in the hope of facilitating broader agreements that would eventually allow it to achieve the long-standing Zionist goal: assured and recognized access to the waters of the Litani River. On both occasions the strategy failed. In 1949 Israel discovered that Lebanon could not make a separate peace; and in 1955 it discovered that an agreement with the states of the Arab League--one which would pave the way for an Israeli-Lebanese accord on the Litani--was equally elusive. Even though one observer thought, in 1955, that Israel's renunciation of its claim to a share of the Litani's waters was tactical in nature and "need not be final,"[20] the water negotiations of the mid-1950s represented Israel's last chance to draw significant amounts of water from Lebanon's largest river. Within a few short years the fundamental assumption upon which Zionist calculations had been based would change.

In June 1954 a report was issued by the U.S. Bureau of Reclamation, whose experts estimated that Lebanon could usefully employ almost all of the Litani's flow for <u>power production</u> as

well as irrigation. The report recommended that Lebanon undertake
a twenty-five-year developmental project that would cost $97.8
million.[21] Israel argued against Lebanon's unilateral use of the
Litani for power production, claiming that the 550-meter drop in
elevation from the Litani to the Jordan Valley was far better
suited for that purpose than the mere 150-meter drop from the
river's westward bend to the Lebanese coastal plain.[22] Yet the
"Litani Project" approved by Beirut in 1955, and based upon the
Bureau of Reclamation's report, did not envision producing
hydroelectric power from the lower course of the Litani. Instead
a dam and reservoir would be constructed at Qir'awn in the
southern Biqa'; tunnels would be blasted through the mountains to
the west; and a large volume of water would be diverted down
through the mountains to the Awwali River, where hydroelectric
power would be produced.

     Beirut's decision to proceed with a comprehensive development
project for the Litani after decades of inaction seems to have
been inspired by Israeli pressure and an insatiable demand for
electricity in the booming metropolis of Beirut. Israel's loudly
voiced complaints that Lebanon was wasting the Litani by allowing
its waters to flow unused into the Mediterranean caused
considerable worry within the Lebanese political elite. Knowing
that the country lacked both the military capability to defend the
south, and the political strength to reach a water-sharing
agreement with Israel, the leaders of Lebanon found themselves
obliged to do something. They elected to try to remove the basis
for Israel's criticism, and to do so in a way beneficial to the
commercial and banking interests of the country. A totally
autonomous power-producing project seemed to be the ideal course
of action.

     When construction began on the Litani Project in 1957, the
plan emphasized hydroelectric production but included provisions
for irrigating "parts of the southern Biqa', scattered patches of
good land in the Galilean Uplands, and parts of the Sidon-Beirut
coastal area."[23] The project evolved, however, into one whose
primary thrust was the provision of electricity to Beirut. This
evolution came about for two reasons: the near-immediate economic
payoff resulting from the production of electricity and southern
Lebanon's lack of influence in the capital. Strong protests by
the political and religious leaders of southern Lebanon eventually
forced Beirut, in the mid-1960s, to adopt a plan whereby enough
water would be provided to irrigate patches of good land south of
the lower Litani, and near the towns of Nabatiyah, Sidon and Marj
'Uyun.[24]

     Phase I of the Litani Project--the hydroelectric phase--was
completed before the start of the June 1967 Arab-Israeli War.[25]
The assumption upon which the Cotton Plan and previous Zionist
plans for using the Litani had been based were dramatically
changed. Whereas Israel had hoped to get 400 million cubic meters
of water from the Litani, the creation of the Qir'awn Dam and
reservoir left only about 100-million cubic meters for the lower

Litani. The very location of the dam and reservoir, well-removed from the frontier region, altered the Zionist assumption that hydroelectric diversions would take place near the border in the vicinity of Marj 'Uyun. Although Qir'awn was one of the places mentioned in the Zionist Statement of February 1919, and was in fact occupied by Israeli forces in 1982, the diversion site was for all practical purposes located in a place where Israel had little permanent interest or influence.

American diplomacy and engineering expertise enabled Lebanon to achieve two very important objectives: the sustaining of a rapid urban economic expansion through the provision of cheap hydroelectric power; and the deflection of Zionist claims to a share of the Litani, claims which had been based to a large degree on the contrast between Zionist need and Lebanese neglect. It was Lebanon's decision to develop its hydroelectric potentialities on its own that blocked Zionist access to the waters of the Litani.

Israel remained determined, with or without Arab cooperation, to divert part of the Jordan River's flow for irrigation purposes. Consequently, in February 1956 a "National Water Carrier Project" for irrigating parts of the Negev Desert was approved, and the scheme was activated in November 1958. In order to avoid armistice complications, the diversion point was shifted from the Banat Ya'qub Bridge to a spot entirely within Israeli territory on the northwestern corner of Lake Tiberias.

Yet so far as the Arab states were concerned, the 1956 Israeli plan was every bit as objectionable as the 1953 scheme. The principle, from the Arab point of view, was the same: "Arab water" from the rivers Hasbani and Banias would flow into the Jordan and eventually be used to support Zionist agricultural colonies in "occupied Palestine." On 30 January 1961 the Political Committee of the Arab League adopted a plan designed to defeat the Israeli National Water Carrier Project. Much to the discomfort of Beirut's political leaders, the plan assigned to Lebanon a very prominent role in the coming confrontation with Israel. The scheme amounted to an attempt to reroute the Arab headwaters of the Jordan--the Hasbani and Banias--away from Israel. The Hasbani would be diverted partially to the west into the lower Litani, with a somewhat smaller quantity going eastward into Syria's Banias River. The Banias would in turn be connected by canal to the Yarmuk River, a tributary of the Jordan forming the boundary between Syria and the Jordanian Kingdom. The effect of the project would be to greatly lower the amount of water flowing into the Jordan Valley between the Israel-Lebanon-Syria triborder area and Lake Tiberias.

Israel's reaction to the project was understandably negative. Noting that the Arab League had earmarked part of the water from the diverted Hasbani for irrigation in southern Lebanon, Israel argued--just as Zionists had argued for decades--that "Lebanon has ample water for irrigation; arable land, not water, has always been the factor limiting the development of Lebanese agriculture."[26] Noting that Lebanon was continuing to "waste"[27] the waters of the Litani, Israel argued that the Arab League diversion scheme

> Would rob the villages in the northern Hula district of the waters of the Hasbani and the Banias which they have been using for centuries. As ancient canals and their ancient names still testify, those waters have been their primary source of irrigation for hundreds of years.
>
> But what is even more serious: the effect of the diversion on Israel would be to diminish, by at least a third, the supply of water to its Lake Kinneret-Negev water project, to cut off the sweet waters of the River Jordan's tributaries, and to add heavily to the salinity of the Lake, which is the intake point of the project, thereby rendering its waters largely unfit for irrigation.[28]

Lebanon, of course, was squarely on the spot. Irrigating the Negev was a venerable Zionist dream, and now Lebanon seemed to be willing to convert its passivity toward Israel into an aggressive program of water denial. In January 1964 the Arab League voted to implement the project, and Lebanon decided to proceed with its share of the undertaking while at the same time declining to invite forces from other Arab states to help defend southern Lebanon. By the early summer of 1965 a track had been leveled from the Hasbani in the direction of the Syrian border, and work had begun on a diversion canal. According to Bar-Yaacov, however, the government of Israel was determined to stop the diversion of the Hasbani even through force if necessary, and such a message was clearly conveyed by Israel to Beirut.[29] Sensing that it had gone quite far enough in demonstrating its "Arabness," Lebanon elected to stop work on the diversion project in July 1965.

Syria continued to work on the Banias diversion site, which from time to time was attacked by Israeli forces. The June 1967 Arab-Israeli war, caused in large part by tensions arising from the water crisis, put a sudden and final end to the Arab League's diversion plan. When the war ended, Israel was in complete possession of the Banias River, the key to the whole scheme. The Hasbani of Lebanon became the only source of the Jordan not located within Israeli-controlled territory.

In a period of only six days, from 5 through 10 June 1967, the amount of territory controlled by the Jewish State tripled. The Golan Heights, the balance of mandatory Palestine, and the entire Sinai Peninsula fell under Israeli military occupation. All of Israel's neighbors, with the notable exception of Lebanon, went to war with their Zionist enemy and lost. In the wake of his country's stunning military success, Defense Minister Moshe Dayan was quoted as stating that Israel had at least achieved "provisionally satisfying frontiers, with the exception of those with Lebanon" Emphasis added . Dayan's statement, coupled with

Israel's renunciation of the 1949 General Armistice Agreement with Lebanon (see Chapter 5 below) led many Lebanese to conclude that Israel intended to "invade and annex a part of Lebanon that would incorporate the Hasbani River."[31]

Had Israel seized the Hasbani in 1967 it would have completed the job of securing the sources of the Jordan River. With the Dan River inside of Israel proper, and the Banias controlled from June 1967 on by Israeli military forces, only the Hasbani lay beyond Israel's grasp. To understand Israel's somewhat bellicose attitude toward Lebanon in the months following June 1967, it must be acknowledged that water disputes had contributed heavily to the tensions which led ultimately to war. From the Israeli perspective Lebanon had not only frustrated Zionist claims to a share of the Litani, but had also gone as far as possible in support of Arab diversion schemes involving the Jordan headwaters. Inasmuch as Syrian-Israeli skirmishing over water diversion projects had helped to ignite the June 1967 war, Israel's position was that Lebanon had indeed played a role--albeit an ineffective one--in making war possible. Viewed in this light, Dayan's statement about the unsatisfactory nature of the Israeli-Lebanese frontier probably reflected two considerations: Israel's desire to ensure that the one remaining source of the Jordan beyond its control would never again be tampered with, and a feeling that Lebanon ought somehow to share in the disastrous consequences suffered by its Arab allies.

Israeli frustration with and antagonism toward Lebanon over the water issue had become apparent in the years immediately preceding the June 1967 war. Three things contributed to Israel's displeasure. First was the issue of the Litani. As Phase I of the Litani Project neared completion in the mid-1960s, Israel realized that the amount of water left for the river's lower course--water that could presumably be diverted to Israel--would be sharply reduced. Zionist exploitation plans which had been first drawn in the early years of the twentieth century would thereby be conclusively nullified. Second was the issue of Arab diversion schemes. Lebanon's decision to see how far it could go in diverting the Hasbani was galling to Israel, particularly when viewed in the light of Lebanon's success in denying Israel access to the Litani. Finally, the questions of the Litani's utilization and the Hasbani's potential diversion were evaluated by Israel's leaders in the context of a third issue: the near total consumption of water available within Israel itself. In 1965 it was estimated that Israel would be using ninety percent of its own water once the National Water Carrier Project was completed.[32] It is no wonder that Lebanese water maneuvers were viewed with neither sympathy nor indifference by Israel.

Israel's irritation with Lebanon became obvious in the course of a parliamentary debate which took place on 8 March 1964, two months after the Arab League had decided to implement its Hasbani River diversion plan. On that day the Knesset witnessed an angry squabble over who was responsible for "losing" the Litani River

after the first Arab-Israeli war. Former Prime Minister Ben
Gurion, eager to advance the political fortunes of his protege,
Moshe Dayan, claimed that Israel would have occupied more
territory in 1948 had Dayan been Chief of Staff at the time. Ben
Gurion's allegation was angrily rebutted by Minister of Labor
Yigal Allon, who said that it was Ben Gurion himself who had
ordered the army to halt when it had been "on the crest of victory
on all vital fronts from the Litani River in the north to the
Sinai desert in the south-west." Just a few more days of
fighting, according to Allon, would have sufficed to "liberate the
entire country."[33] Although the debate had more to do with
internal Israeli political rivalries than anything else, it
nevertheless suggested that Israel's leaders—all of whom
participated in the 1948 war—had, by the mid-1960s, developed
profound regrets over not having adjusted the frontier with
Lebanon when the opportunity existed. Those regrets had
undoubtedly been prompted by the contrast between Israeli water
requirements on the one hand, and Lebanese maneuvers with regard
to the Hasbani and Litani on the other. By 1967 Prime Minister
Eshkol of Israel was publicly resurrecting the age-old allegation
that Lebanon was wasting the precious water of the Litani by
allowing it to run into the sea.[34]

By renouncing the armistice agreement and declaring the
Lebanese frontier to be less than satisfying, Israel seemed in
1967 to be seriously considering an adjustment of its boundary
with Lebanon. Indeed, Michael Hudson reported in 1970 that "since
the June war Israeli officials had gone out of their way to
communicate to Lebanon that the 1949 armistice was no longer
binding."[35] There appear to be two reasons why Israel ultimately
chose not to occupy Lebanese territory during or after the 1967
war. First, the renunciation of the General Armistice Agreement
had to do only partly with the festering water issue between the
two countries. It was also designed to solidify Israel's legal
status with regard to its continued military occupation of Arab
lands conquered in 1967. Second, the water issue itself lost much
of its urgency in the months and years following June 1967. On
the one hand the diversion of large quantities of Litani water at
Qir'awn became a _fait accompli_ about which Israel could do very
little. Second, with the seizure of the Banias stream by Israel
in June 1967, the prospects of the Hasbani's ever being diverted
became nil. Lebanon had been severely chastened by the spectacle
of the six-day war, and it was obviously in no position to
threaten the supply of water to the upper Jordan Valley. An
Israeli seizure of southern Lebanon could have provoked
international outrage and condemnation without significantly
enhancing Israel's economic prospects.

By October 1968 the water controversy, a dispute which had
led to the third Arab-Israeli war, and which for two decades had
imperiled Lebanon's sovereignty over the southern districts, had
faded considerably. In its place was a more deadly confrontation,
one which would eventually bring Lebanon itself to destruction.
The advent of _fedayeen_ commando activity in the frontier area

served to completely change the focus of the Israeli-Lebanese relationship from water to security. Perhaps nothing better illustrates this change than an incident which occurred during the height of the Lebanese civil war. The Christian town of Marj 'Uyun, cut off from the rest of Lebanon by severe fighting, had developed economic ties with Israel. A water pipeline was eventually laid, linking the Lebanese town with an Israeli settlement. When the water was finally turned on, one of the great ironies of the Israeli-Lebanese relationship transpired. Notwithstanding the long, bitter, and controversial history of Zionist demands for a share of Lebanon's water, the water flowing in the Marj 'Uyun pipeline came not from Lebanon for use by Jewish farmers in the Negev, but from Israel for the relief of beleaguered Lebanese villagers.[36]

Although some commentators still see traditional Zionist claims on Lebanese water as an important motivating factor behind Israel's involvement in Lebanon,[37] there is no evidence that the Israelis have done anything to procure water from the Lebanese territory they now occupy. Instead it appears that the policy of Israel toward Lebanon has in recent years far more to do with broader geopolitical considerations involving the Palestine Liberation Organization and the nature of the Lebanese state. Yet even though water seems no longer to be the key determinant in Israel's approach to the problems of southern Lebanon, there is no question that the frustrations and defeats suffered by Zionism over the water issue between 1923 and 1968 served only to increase the bitterness engendered by the initial Anglo-French boundary compromise. It seems reasonable to suggest that the prolonged Zionist frustration over the issue of water contributed to the violent tenor of subsequent Israeli actions in southern Lebanon, even though the proximate reason for Israeli violence in southern Lebanon was _fedayeen_ violence against targets in Israel. To the extent that Zionist frustration over water helped to dictate Israel's subsequent attitude toward southern Lebanon, Beirut's "victory" in the water controversy was quite costly indeed.

NOTES

1. Abraham H. Hirsch, "Utilization of International Rivers in the Middle East," _American Journal of International Law_, Volume 50, Number 1, January 1956, p. 88.

2. Sa'id B. Himadeh, ed., _Economic Organization of Syria_ (Beirut: American University of Beirut, 1936), p. 43.

3. James Hudson, "The Litani River of Lebanon: An Example of Middle Eastern Water Development," _Middle East Journal_, Volume 25, No. 1, Winter 1971, p. 7.

4. Hedley V. Cooke, <u>Challenge and Response in the Middle East</u> (New York: Harper & Brothers, 1952), p. 137.

5. Ibid., p. 139.

6. H. F. Frischwasser-Ra'anan, <u>The Frontiers of a Nation</u> (London: The Batchworth Press, 1955), p. 139.

7. Basim A. Faris, <u>Electric Power in Syria and Palestine</u> (Beirut: American University of Beirut, 1936), p. 292.

8. Dana Adams Schmidt, "Prospects for a Solution of the Jordan River Dispute," <u>Middle Eastern Affairs</u>, Volume VI, Number 1, January 1955, p. 4.

9. Charles Issawi, "Economic Development and Liberalism in Lebanon," <u>Middle East Journal</u>, Volume 18, Number 3, Summer 1964, p. 285.

10. Don Peretz, "Development of the Jordan Valley Waters," <u>Middle East Journal</u>, Volume 9, Number 4, Autumn 1955, p. 406.

11. Samir N. Saliba, <u>The Jordan River Dispute</u> (The Hague: Martinus Nijhoff, 1968), p. 45.

12. Earl Berger, <u>The Covenant and the Sword</u> (London: Routledge & Kegan Paul Ltd., 1965), p. 30.

13. Schmidt, "Prospects for a Solution of the Jordan River Dispute," p. 5.

14. Ibid., p. 10.

15. Michael Brecher, <u>Decisions in Israel's Foreign Policy</u> (New Haven: Yale University Press, 1975), p. 197.

16. Hudson. "The Litani River of Lebanon," p. 13.

17. Peretz, "Development of the Jordan River Waters," p. 406.

18. Hudson, "The Litani River of Lebanon," p. 13.

19. Peretz, "Development of the Jordan River Waters," pp. 409-419.

20. Schmidt, "Prospects for a Solution of the Jordan River Dispute," p. 10.

21. Ibid.

22. Ibid.

23. Hudson, "The Litani River of Lebanon," p. 8.

24. Ibid., p. 11.

25. John L. Cooley, "Lebanon Fears Loss of Water to Israel," Christian Science Monitor, 23 March 1978, p. 3.

26. "The Arab Plan to Divert the Headwaters of the River Jordan," Ministry of Foreign Affairs (Jerusalem), April 1965, in Yoneh Alexander and Nicholas N. Kittrie, eds., Crescent and Star: Arab and Israeli Perspectives on the Middle East Conflict (New York: AMS Press, Inc., 1973), p. 289.

27. Ibid.

28. Ibid., pp. 288-289.

29. N. Bar-Yaacov, The Israel-Syrian Armistice (Jerusalem: Magnes Press, 1967), p. 148.

30. Cooley, "Lebanon Fears Loss of Water to Israel," p. 3.

31. Paul A. Jureidini and William E. Hazen, The Palestinian Movement in Politics (Lexington: D.C, Health and Company, 1976), p. 59.

32. "The Arab Plan to Divert the Headwaters of the River Jordan," p. 289.

33. "Dispute Over Size of Israel," Times (London), 9 March 1964, p. 8.

34. Cooley, "Lebanon Fears Loss of Water to Israel," p. 3.

35. Michael Hudson, "Fedayeen Are Forcing Lebanon's Hand," Mid East Vol. X, Number 1, February 1970, p. 7.

36. Helena Cobban, "S. Lebanon: Integration with Israel?" Christian Science Monitor, 9 November 1977, p. 34.

37. See Hasan Sharif, "South Lebanon: Its History and Geopolitics," in South Lebanon, edited by Elaine Hagopian and Samih Farsoun (Detroit: Association of Arab-American University Graduates, 1978), p. 21. Sharif believes that use of Lebanese waters is the quid pro quo that Israel will exact for its assistance to Lebanese rightists, and that the rightists have already acceded to Israel's desire. This agreement, according to Sharif, is "A well-propagated 'secret' among the Lebanese." No evidence is offered, however, to document the existence of such an "agreement."

5. Evolving Security Problems: 1925–1949

During negotiations which led to the Franco-British Convention of 23 December 1920, Dr. Weizmann and his colleagues based their case for the northern boundary exclusively on economic grounds. This is not to say, however, that they were unconcerned about the military defense of Palestine; indeed, the Tel Hai incident of March 1920 gave substance to their fears. Although the Zionists were unable to openly debate the location of suitable defensible terrain in Upper Galilee -- Great Britain and France being officially allies --there is no question that the security aspect was considered. In November 1919 Colonel Richard Meinertzhagen, General Allenby's ardently pro-Zionist (though non-Jewish) Chief Political Officer in Palestine, made a boundary proposal of his own which may also have represented the Zionist counter to the Deauville Proposal (see page no. above). The "Meinertzhagen Line," depicted on Figure 5.1, would have anchored the northern defense of Palestine on the Litani River in the west and center, and in a chain of hills dividing the Biqa' and Marj valleys in the east.[1] Yet Great Britain and France instead contrived a boundary that proved to be easily penetrable by small armed forces at almost any point.

Between 1924 and 1936 the Palestine-Lebanon boundary was unfenced, virtually unguarded, and extremely quiet. Zionist misgivings about a boundary that offered almost no defensible terrain seemed to have been rendered irrelevant by two things: friendly relations between Great Britain and France, which were fully reflected in the benign relationship between Palestine and Lebanon; and the sensibly flexible frontier regulations embodied in the 1926 "good neighbourly relations" accord. The boundary between the two Levantine states posed no particular problem to either of the mandatory powers.

There was, however, one disquieting chain of events in southern Lebanon that foreshadowed future unpleasantness. It had to do with the arming of a Christian militia in southern Lebanon in 1925 and its employment against fellow Arabs. Stephen Longrigg's observations concerning the events of 1925 evoke an echo over a half-century later:

> Whatever the admitted shortage of regular troops, and the urgent pleas of defenseless Christians, the result could never be to produce effective or reliable auxiliaries, but always to prejudice the future by increasing ill-feeling, and sometimes vendetta, between Christian and Muslim, from which the former must be the greater sufferers.[2]

A rebellion against France had erupted in the Jabal Druze region of Syria in late 1925 and quickly spilled over the border into southern Lebanon. After taking the Druze village of Hasbaya,

FIGURE 5.1: THE "MEINERTZHAGEN LINE,"
NOVEMBER 1919

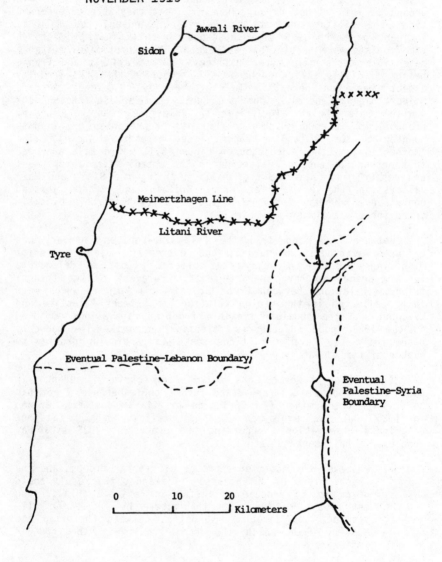

the Druze rebels occupied the Christian towns of Kawkaba and Marj 'Uyun. France, which had a skeletal security force in Lebanon and virtually nothing in the south, capitalized on traditional Maronite-Druze antipathy by arming the Christian villagers of southern Lebanon. The rebellion ran out of steam in Lebanon when the insurgents failed to capture the non-Christian towns of Nabatiyah and Rashayya.

The Christians of southern Lebanon viewed the Druze incursion not as an attack on France but as an armed assault on their own community. The fighting of 1925 "drove terrified Christians in thousands from their village homes,"[3] an event facilitated no doubt by memories of ancestral experiences with the Druze. The rebels had hoped to obtain the "friendly neutrality" of the Christians, but sectarian violence in Kawkaba made that an impossibility.[4] Although the uprising never touched Palestine, it reinforced the tendency of the outnumbered Christians on the Lebanese side of the border to view politics largely in terms of communal survival, and to reach out if necessary for assistance from non-Arabs in order to fight other Arabs. Yet according to one contemporary account of the campaign in southern Lebanon, France's employment of untrained Christian volunteers helped to insure the early loss of Marj 'Uyun to the rebels and constituted a "political disaster."

> By calling upon one community in the mandated territory to take up arms against another the mandatory Power intensified the traditional blood-feuds between Syrian communities of different religions and thus actually worked against the purpose of the mandatory regime, which had been intended to educate the Syrians in the art of cooperation as an essential step towards self-government.[5]

The events of 1925 confirmed the isolation of the Christian minority in southern Lebanon, and foreshadowed the eventual collaboration of that Christian community with Israel's efforts to secure its northern boundary.

Although the Druze rebellion did not spill over into Jewish settlements in Palestine, growing tensions between Zionism and Arab nationalism eventually caused a change in conditions along the boundary and resurrected Zionist worries about the defense of northern Palestine. In April 1936 a series of Arab uprisings began in Palestine, disturbances caused by "(i) The desire of the Arabs for national independence and (ii) Their hatred and fear of the establishment of the Jewish National Home."[6] There was much sympathy for the Arab revolt in the states bordering Palestine, and in time the regions contiguous to Palestine became staging areas and sanctuaries for bands of Palestinian Arab guerrillas.

Within Lebanon the district of Bint Jubayl became the area "most notoriously utilized for the passage of aid to the insurgents."[7]   The British authorities, finding themselves completely incapable of stemming the flow of men and materiel from Lebanon and Syria, appealed to the French officials for assistance. The British discovered, as would the Israelis some three decades later, that an effective military defense of Palestine would have to begin in southern Lebanon; that the political boundary itself was completely open to infiltration from the north. The British also discovered, as would the Israelis in the fullness of time, that the authorities in Beirut were none too eager to lend a helping hand. As one contemporary account explained,

> Efforts made by the Palestine Government to obtain the cooperation of the French mandatory authorities...have been unsuccessful. The French have given over much of the detail of government to the Syrian and Lebanese States, whose sympathy with the Palestinian Arab Nationalists in the one case and fear of antagonizing the French in the other prevent them from doing anything.[8]

Put differently, France had no desire to touch off another rebellion in Syria by helping the British quell the Arab uprising in Palestine. The Lebanese authorities, not wishing to create difficulties either for their French patrons or themselves (by stirring up Arab nationalist sentiment within Lebanon), simply ignored the use to which their southern districts were being put.

Unable to seal the border, and unable to secure French or Lebanese cooperation, the British were forced to act unilaterally. "Unofficial" raids were launched against Arab villages through Lebanese territory by Jewish commandos led by a British officer, Orde Wingate.[9] These raids may have helped the future military leaders of Israel overcome any reservations about conducting military operations on Lebanese territory. In 1937 the Inspector-General of the Palestine Police, R.G.B. Spicer, proposed that the country's land borders be physically sealed. His recommendation was shelved due to the anticipated cost of the undertaking, but worsening security conditions caused the idea to reappear in 1938 as a recommendation by Sir Charles Tegart, security advisor to the Palestine government. Tegart's proposal was accepted on 1 May.[10]

A contract worth 90,000 pounds sterling was awarded to the Jewish firm of Soleh Boneh, Ltd., of Haifa to construct a barrier along Palestine's borders with Lebanon, Syria, and Transjordan. Along the Lebanese border, the specifications called for a barrier consisting of two or three (depending upon the terrain) barbed-wire fences, with tangled wire between each fence. The wall itself would be guarded by the frontier posts already existing, with additional pillboxes to be constructed in areas where footpaths crossed the boundary.[11] Even before construction was finished the edifice came to be known as "Tegart's Wall."

The wall was built during the months of May and June 1938. Its objective was to strictly regulate the passage of human traffic between Palestine and Lebanon along the entire length of the common border. It failed quite miserably. Instead of improving the security of Palestine, Tegart's Wall spread rebellion to the frontier zone itself. Instead of immunizing Palestine from the activities of outsiders, it united Arab peasants on both sides of the boundary in a violent campaign against the wall and against the British security forces trying to guard it. A newspaper account of the problem, printed in July 1938, gave the following assessment of the wall's impact:

> Intended to be no more than an obstacle which would slow up the passage of bandits and contraband arms, this fence has stirred up the wrath of villagers on both sides of the frontier because it has bisected village lands, interfered with normal pasturage, and erected for the first time an artificial barrier to the trade, both legal and contraband, which has gone on between adjacent villages from time immemorial. Attacks on the "Wall" became so difficult to control that a special military force was posted along it at the end of June.[12]

The 800-man Rural Mounted Police force dispatched to guard the fence was simply no match for the anger of Lebanese and Palestinian Arab peasants. The authorities in Jerusalem were obliged to impose curfews on the Arab villages of the Acre and Safed subdistricts near the Lebanese border,[13] but resistance to Tegart's Wall was too intense to be overcome without French cooperation.

The disastrous effects of Tegart's Wall induced Great Britain to redouble its efforts to secure French assistance. Eventually France agreed to field a 1,000-man unit to patrol the Lebanese and Syrian boundaries with Palestine, a force consisting of four squadrons of horse cavalry and two squadrons of mechanized cavalry.[14] The French effort, belated though it was, succeeded in impeding raids launched from Lebanon. In the end, however, it was a political accomodation rather than Anglo-French security operations that restored tranquility to the frontier area. The Arab revolt itself ended in 1939, when Great Britain issued a White Paper that did much to placate the fundamental Arab grievances over Zionist expansion in Palestine.[15] Left undefended, Tegart's Wall was rapidly dismantled.

Three significant lessons were learned from Britain's experience with a physical barrier along the Palestine-Lebanon boundary. First, Zionist qualms about the military-geographic deficiencies of the border proved to be well-justified. The 1920 Anglo-French compromise had sought to assuage Zionist fears through the simple expedient of drawing a boundary line around the northernmost Jewish settlements, the unspoken assumption being that British sovereignty itself would be an adequate security guarantee. The real problem uncovered during the period 1936-1939, however, was that northern Palestine was penetrable almost everywhere. This revelation—which had actually figured in

Zionist boundary calculations from the beginning--helped to reinforce that dimension of Zionist thinking that viewed the Litani River not only as a potential economic asset, but as a natural defensive obstacle as well.

The second lesson had to do with the residents of the Palestine-Lebanon frontier zone. If geographic homogeneity made border security difficult, ethnic homogeneity made it impossible. The existence of a preponderantly Arab population on both sides of the boundary not only facilitated infiltration, but frustrated British attempts to deal with the situation. During the 1930s Arabs comprised about ninety percent of the population of the Safed subdistrict of Palestine and ninety-nine percent of Palestine's Acre subdistrict.[16] Furthermore, as late as 1944 Arabs held eighty-two percent of the land in the former subdistrict and ninety-seven percent in the latter.[17] By 1946 the total Jewish population for both subdistricts bordering Lebanon was a mere 10,000.[18] Throughout the mandate period, therefore, the frontier region remained almost entirely Arab, and cross-border contacts remained intact despite the political boundary. As Sharif has pointed out, "many families had branches in villages on both sides of the border. Indeed it was difficult to find a family that did not have a relative on the other side."[19] Arab solidarity in the border area was conclusively demonstrated by the negative public reaction to the imposition of a fence along the border, an obstacle which threatened patterns of life in the Upper Galilee in an unprecedented manner. The security implications of the public outcry against Tegart's Wall were therefore clear: unless the Arabs living on each side of the line could be induced to develop mutually exclusive national loyalties, then the ethnic homogeneity of the area would forever preclude the effective closing of the border by any non-Arab regime in Jerusalem. Unless that homogeneity could be broken, northern Palestine would always constitute a security nightmare for any authority seeking to pursue policies contrary to the aspirations of the Arabs in the frontier zone. Even with the severe military-geographic handicaps presented by the frontier, an organized defense of northern Palestine could be undertaken by non-Arab forces provided the people on one side of the line were clearly different from the people on the other side.

Finally, the use of Lebanese territory as a sanctuary and staging area, combined with the initial absence of French/Lebanese cooperation with the British, provided a lesson for the future. Beirut's lack of initiative in 1938, a prudent course of inaction designed to placate both Lebanese and Syrian supporters of the Arab rebellion in Palestine, gave the guerrilla bands complete freedom of action for a limited period of time. Great Britain was in no position to force French cooperation and was obliged instead to build a barrier which only exacerbated the security problem. Had the two countries not been nominal allies, it is quite possible that the British would have assigned responsibility for the deteriorating security situation to Beirut and undertaken retaliatory operations on Lebanese soil. Indeed, such a policy would eventually be followed by Israel when faced with Arab commandos operating from neighboring countries -- a policy of retaliation applied not only to Lebanon but to Syria, Jordan, and Egypt as well.

The events of 1936-1939 enabled the Zionists to give serious thoughts to the very weighty security problems presented by the boundary drawn for Palestine and Lebanon by Great Britain and France. Within a very short period of time Zionist military personnel would be given the opportunity to conduct combat operations in southern Lebanon, operations that would yield valuable data on how to "defend" the Jewish Homeland from the vantage point of Lebanese territory.

Peace had barely been restored to the Palestine-Lebanon frontier when events in Europe suddenly put an end to the officially harmonious relationship between the mandatory regimes in Beirut and Jerusalem. France fell to Nazi Germany in April 1940, and a collaborationist French government was installed at Vichy. Lebanon and Syria were governed by an administration which opted to remain loyal to Vichy, thus putting the French Levant at odds with British Palestine. Great Britain viewed the Vichy presence in the Middle East as an opening for Germany and began quickly to formulate plans for the invasion of Lebanon and Syria. General de Gaulle's Free French were apprised of the British plans so as to still the inevitable French fear that Great Britain's real objective was to supplant the French imperial presence in Beirut and Damascus with its own. An invasion plan was eventually formulated and named "Operation Exporter."[20]

On 30 June 1940 the Palestine-Lebanon border was partly closed by the British authorities. On 25 May 1941 it was officially closed.[21] Although the effect that these administrative measures may have had on the peasants of Upper Galilee is not known, it is likely that the only area really affected by the border closure was the official crossing point at Ras an Naqurah. In any event Operation Exporter began on 8 June 1941. Although the campaign included an attack on Damascus (as well as Dayr az Zawr on the Euphrates), this discussion will be restricted to the operation's main thrust, which was an invasion of Lebanon launched from Palestine.

The main objective of Operation Exporter was Beirut. The attacking force consisted of two infantry brigades of the 7th Australian Division and one battalion of Jewish commandos. Opposing the invasion was a French ground force of roughly equal strength. However, the Australians possessed significant air and naval advantages.[22]

Geography limited the Australians to two axes of advance into Lebanon: the coastal road to Beirut, and straight up the Biqa' Valley to the Beirut-Damascus Highway. Both axes channeled the attackers into narrow corridors, thereby offering a significant terrain advantage to the defense. Yet the Australians had little

choice.   An attack across the boundary between the coast and
Metulla would have to contend with the twisted terrain of Jabal
'Amil.   Furthermore, the coastal axis would give the Australians
the opportunity to exploit one of their few clear advantages: a
monopoly on supporting naval gunfire.

On 8 June the Australians seized the Lebanese border post at
Ra's an Naqurah and began to move north.   The supporting attack
succeeded in taking Marj 'Uyun on 11 June.   Yet problems quickly
developed.   On 10 June a unit of Jewish commandos, trained by the
British, conducted an unsuccessful assault on the Qasimiyyah
coastal bridge.   A young commando named Moshe Dayan lost his left
eye during the attack.   Fearing that the main (coastal) attack
would bog down, the supporting attack up the Biqa' was aborted in
favor of a turn toward the coast by way of Marj 'Uyun and Jazzin.
A skeletal force was left behind to garrison Marj 'Uyun, which was
promptly retaken by the Vichy forces on 16 June while the bulk of
the supporting brigade became hopelessly entangled in the
mountains of southern Lebanon.   That particular unit never made it
to the coast, becoming instead completely bogged down.[23]

The Vichy forces in Marj 'Uyun had insufficient strength to
attack Palestine through Metulla, and the Australians recaptured
the town on 24 June.   Meanwhile the main attack, using air and
naval superiority, simply bludgeoned its way to the outskirts of
Beirut.   An armistice was signed on 14 July 1941, ending Vichy
rule in the Levant.

Scarcely a footnote to the history of the Second World War,
Operation Exporter nevertheless taught the embryonic Jewish
military leadership in Palestine about military operations in
southern Lebanon.   Operation Exporter was a practical
demonstration of the problems faced by Palestine in connection
with the military geography of the border region.   Whereas
Palestine was open to infiltration from Lebanon at almost any
point, conventional axes of advance into Lebanon were few.   In
fact, given parity in air and indirect fire support, the Vichy
French surely would have defeated both Australian attacks.   Given
the existence of only two potential "high-speed" approaches into
Lebanon -- the coastal road and the Metulla-Marj 'Uyun-Biqa' route
-- and the preponderance of secondary roads running east-west
rather than north-south, it can be concluded that given forces of
roughly equal strength, a virtually insurmountable defensive
advantage accrues to the force facing south.   Furthermore, the
momentary threat of an invasion of Palestine when the Vichy forces
took Marj 'Uyun may well have left behind a residue of concern
about the potential offensive threat from the north, a "threat"
which nevertheless would face many of the same difficulties
connected with offensive operations directed toward the north.

The experiences associated with Tegart's Wall and Operation
Exporter seemed, therefore, to yield contradictory prescriptive
concepts.   From the Zionist perspective, would it be better to
have southern Lebanon garrisoned by sizeable numbers of Lebanese

security personnel so as to control and dissuade irregular crossborder operations against targets inside Palestine? That seemed to be the lesson drawn from the events of 1936-1939. Or would it be better for Zionist military planners if southern Lebanon were very thinly garrisoned, thereby insuring the success of offensive or retaliatory operations launched from Palestine into Lebanon while at the same time insuring against the possibility of conventional attack from Lebanon? Such a conclusion would be rational in the light of Operation Exporter. Still another possibility may have occurred to the Jewish military leaders: commando raids into Palestine fully supported by Lebanese authorities and backed up by a strong conventional force in the south. As it happened, the terms of the 1949 armistice between Israel and Lebanon, signed after the end of the first Arab-Israeli war, limited the Lebanese Army to a mere 1,500 soldiers in an area roughly defined as everything south of the Qasimiyyah (Litani) River.

Shortly after World-War-II, Levantine politics became transfixed once again on the clash between Arabs and Zionists over the future of Palestine. Great Britain found its position as mandatory power untenable, and following its failure in February 1947 to negotiate an Arab-Zionist accommodation, it called upon the United Nations to deal with the question of Palestine. On 29 November 1947 the General Assembly approved a resolution which called for "dividing Palestine into Arab and Jewish states which were to remain in economic union and the establishment of a special international regime for the City of Jerusalem."[25] The resolution was rejected by the Arab states, which undertook by force to prevent its implementation.

Had the partition resolution of November 1947 ever been implemented, its impact on the Palestine-Lebanon frontier would have been considerable. According to the terms of the resolution, that part of the 1923 boundary extending from the Mediterranean coast at Ras an Naqurah across to a point just north of the Palestinian village of Saliha would have been under the jurisdiction of the Arab State. Along the coast the Arab jurisdiction would have extended from Ras an Naqurah south to Acre, and inland the northern portion of the Arab State would have reached south to a point just below the town of Nazareth.[26] Figure 5.2 shows how the Palestine side of the frontier zone would have been affected by implementation of the partition resolution. It is worth noting that nearly the entire subdistrict of Safed--an area which figured so prominently in the post-World-War-I Anglo-French boundary negotiations because of the presence of Jewish settlements--was set aside for inclusion in the proposed Jewish State, despite the presence of a preponderantly Arab population in the subdistrict.

Arab opposition ensured, however, that the partition resolution would never be implemented. As the British mandate drew to a close in May 1948, conditions along the Palestine-Lebanon boundary reverted to the chaotic state that had prevailed

FIGURE 5.2: EFFECT OF THE 1947
PARTITION RESOLUTION

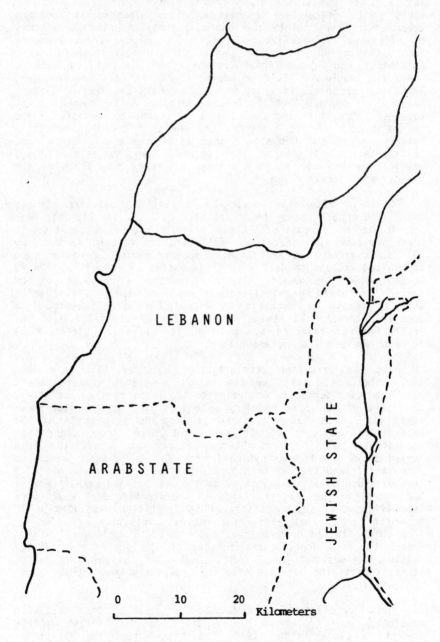

LEBANON

ARABSTATE

JEWISH STATE

0   10   20
⊢————⊢————⊢ Kilometers

during the Arab uprising of 1936-1939. An Arab guerrilla band known as the Arab Liberation Army, under the leadership of Fawzi al-Qawuqji (a veteran of the 1936 Arab uprising), operated on both sides of the border in the Upper Galilee. Southern Lebanon, now part of the independent Republic of Lebanon, again served as a sanctuary and staging area for Arab raiders.

As was the case one decade earlier, Lebanon was disinclined to interfere with commando operations against targets in Palestine launched from its southern districts. Like the other Arab countries, Lebanon harbored serious doubts that an autonomous Arab state would ever emerge in partitioned Palestine. Furthermore, like its sister Arab governments, Lebanon entertained the notion of gaining some territory at Palestine's expense. Beirut decided, therefore, to use the Lebanese Army to support and supply Qawuqji's forces "in the hope that if there was to be a carve-up of Arab Palestine, she at least might lay claim to the Upper Galilee."[27] There were, however, limits to the extent of Lebanon's armed commitment to the "rescue" of Palestine. With a small army tailored to the requirements of maintaining internal security, Lebanon was in no positon to conduct sustained offensive operations in Palestine. Its military involvement in the struggle for Palestine was largely symbolic, an attempt to derive maximum political and territorial gains from minimal military efforts.

From the point of view of the Zionist military leadership, there were three avenues of approach leading from Lebanon into Palestine: on the left from Ras an Naqurah straight down the coast toward Acre; in the center from the vicinity of Bint Jubayl to any number of border crossing points; and on the right through the Hula Valley by way of Marj 'Uyun and Metulla.[28] Yet, as Sacher has pointed out, "The lines of communication were not...favorable to the attack. As the roads across Galilee ran west and east and not from north to south, an advance from Lebanon was handicapped."[29] Aside from occupying the Palestinian border post at Ras an Naqurah on 24 May 1948, the Lebanese Army's involvement in the first Arab-Israeli war was limited to the Bint Jubayl sector of the frontier. On 15 May 1948, Israel's first day as a self-proclaimed independent state, two Lebanese infantry battalions and a company of armor attacked and overran the tiny settlement of Malkiya.[30] The seizure of Malkiya formally placed Lebanon in opposition to the U.N. partition plan for Palestine, as the settlement was located in an area designated by the U.N. as part of the projected Jewish State.

Three days later Israel launched a counterattack. A small motorized Israeli force entered Lebanon near the hamlet of Al 'Udaysah, some eighteen kilometers north of the Malkiya crossing point. The Israeli force drove south within Lebanese territory past the hamlets of Markaba, Hula, Mays al Jabal, and Blida. South of Blida the Israelis turned southeast and reentered Palestine, taking the small Lebanese garrison by surprise and recapturing Malkiya from the rear.[31]

FIGURE 5.3: LEBANESE TERRITORY
OVERRUN BY ISRAELIS (SHADED AREA)

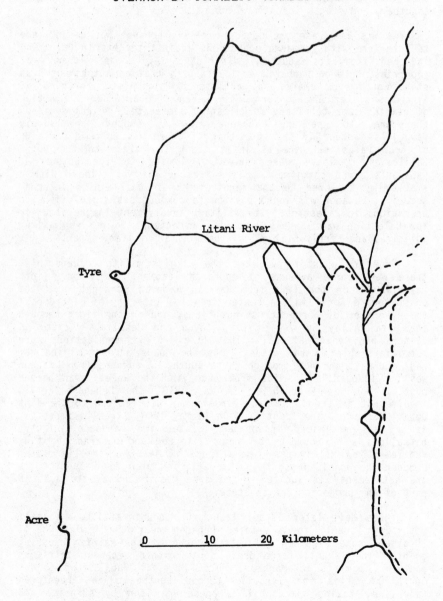

The Lebanese Army reacted to the loss of Malkiya by conducting, on 6 June 1948, its only real combat operation of the war. Malkiya was successfully stormed, and another small settlement, Kadesh-Naftali, was overrun on the next day. According to O'Ballance,

> This assault on Malkiya was the solitary Lebanese success of the war, and it consisted of an infantry attack by about 800 men, with only mortar support. Not much can be deduced from this action as the victory was perhaps as much due to overwhelming numbers as to any other factor.[32]

Lebanon was not, however, emboldened in the least by its apparent prowess on the battlefield. After the victory at Malkiya it prudently retired from active participation in the war, turning over its gains in the central sector to the Arab Liberation Army. At the end of the first Arab-Israeli truce (9 July 1948) Lebanese forces in the frontier region were deployed at Bint Jubayl and a few meters across the border in the "Arab" sector of Palestine at Ras an Naqurah.[33]

Lebanon found, however, that disengagement from the war in Palestine was no simple matter. Israeli forces, intent upon securing as much of mandatory Palestine as possible, launched a campaign in October 1948 designed to clear the Arab Liberation Army from northern Palestine. "Operation Hiram," named after the ancient King of Tyre, was an unqualified Israeli success. The Arab Liberation Army was forced to abandon Palestine and retreated into the Lebanese district of Bint Jubayl. Israeli forces pursued the enemy into Lebanon, where (according to an Israeli observer) they "were molested less by Kaoukji's men than by aggressive Levantine salesmen armed with fountain pens, nylons, and souvenir trinkets from the markets of Beirut and Tyre."[34] The Lebanese Army judiciously refrained from taking a stand against the invading Israelis, and the Jewish forces found themselves in control of eighteen Lebanese villages in an area "running parallel to the Manara road up to Wadi Duba and the Litani River, which geographically and historically marked the boundary of Upper Galilee."[35] Figure 5.3 depicts the extent of Israel's occupation of Lebanese territory at the end of the first Arab-Israeli war.

At last the Zionists had secured a foothold on the Litani River, and there was at first every indication that they intended to keep it. In late 1948, claims emanated from Israeli diplomatic and journalistic circles to the effect that the occupied Lebanese villages were asking to be placed under Israeli military authority, and that there was a pro-Zionist "free Lebanese movement" active in Israel.[36] It appeared that some public relations groundwork was being done to justify the outright annexation of Lebanese territory by Israel.

Instead of changing its northern boundary, however, Israel adopted the strategy of trading land for political concessions.

The leaders of Israel believed in early 1949 that they could conclude a very attractive peace settlement with the Christian-dominated Lebanese state. Presumably such a treaty would not only secure for Israel access to the waters of the Litani but would further fragment the Arab world by detaching Lebanon from the Arab coalition. On 21 May 1948 David Ben Gurion, the first Prime Minister of Israel, made the following entry in his diary:

> The Achilles' heel of the Arab coalition is the Lebanon. Muslim supremacy in this country is artificial and can easily be overthrown. A Christian State ought to be set up there, with its southern frontier on the River Litani. We would sign a treaty of alliance with this state.[37]

Evidently, Israeli negotiators decided that they could have either the Litani or a treaty, but not both. Consequently, when armistice talks with Lebanon under U.N. auspices began in January 1949, Israel displayed a willingness bordering on eagerness to part with territory, as it quickly withdrew from four of the occupied Lebanese villages in return for a minuscule Lebanese pullback from the Israeli side of Ras an Naqurah.[38] However, several weeks of stalemate followed, as Israel tried to couple its withdrawal from Lebanon with a Syrian withdrawal from a tiny piece of Palestinian territory in the Hula Valley. The issues were eventually separated, however, and on 23 March 1949 a General Armistice Agreement (GAA) between Israel and Lebanon was signed.

The GAA was not a peace treaty. It left Lebanon and Israel in a technical state of war, even through Israel regarded its signing as "the penultimate step towards peace."[39] Israeli forces withdrew from Lebanon behind an Armistice Demarcation Line (ADL), the purpose of which was to "delineate the line beyond which the armed forces of the respective parties shall not move."[40] As to the location of the ADL, the GAA provided that "The Armistice Demarcation Line shall follow the international boundary between the Lebanon and Palestine."[41]

Not only did the GAA restore the 1923 boundary in the form of an armistice line, but it established specific military limitations to be observed on both sides of the ADL. The text of the GAA called for the stationing of "defensive forces only" in the "region of the Armistice Demarcation Line."[42] "Defensive forces" were defined as follows in the Annex to the GAA:

1. In the case of the Lebanon:

> Two battalions and two companies of Lebanese Regular Army Infantry, one field battery of 4 guns and one company of 12 light armoured cars armed with machineguns and 6 light tanks armed with light guns (20 vehicles). Total 1,500 officers and enlisted men.

(ii) No other military forces, than those mentioned in (i) shall be employed south of the general line El-Qasmiye-Nabatiye ett Tahta-Hasbaya.

2. In the case of Israel:

(i) One infantry battalion, one support company with six mortars and six machineguns, with six armoured cars and one reconnaissance company, six armoured jeeps, one battalion of field artillery with four guns, one platoon of field engineers and service units such as Quartermaster and Ordnance, total not to exceed 1,500 officers and enlisted men.

(ii) No other military forces, than those mentioned in 2(i) above, shall be employed north of the general line Nahariya-Tarshiya-Jish-Marus.[43]

Thus, the "region of the Armistice Demarcation Line" amounted to the virtual demilitarization of southern Lebanon. Figure 5.4 depicts the limited-forces zone agreed upon by the two sides. It will be noticed that on the Lebanese side of the ADL offensive forces were prohibited not only south of the Litani River but south of Nabatiyah, a full seven kilometers north of the river. The point at which offensive forces could be closest to Israel was approximately twelve kilometers north of Metulla near the village of Balat.

In Israel the limited-forces line was drawn much closer to the ADL near the Mediterranean end of the boundary than was the corresponding line in Lebanon, but at its eastern terminus it was much further from Lebanon than was the Lebanese limited-forces line from Israel. Under the terms of the GAA it would be clearly permissible for Israel to concentrate the bulk of its offensive forces in the Hula Valley region, where it also had Syrians to contend with, and still have unlimited forces behind a line only ten kilometers south of the Lebanese boundary from the Mediterranean coast to the vicinity of Malkiya, where the boundary turned sharply to the north. Furthermore, the GAA said nothing whatever about paramilitary forces being stationed in newly created Jewish settlements being build right up against the ADL.

If the demilitarization of southern Lebanon eased Israeli anxiety about the possibility of a conventional military threat from the north, the demographic transformation of northern Israel was seen as at least a partial answer to the problem of irregular warfare. Thousands of Arabs fled to Lebanon from northern Palestine during the fighting of 1948, and their abandoned villages abutting the Lebanese border were converted into armed Israeli settlements. During the years 1948-50 many such settlements were established, and Arabs still living near the border were relocated for security purposes.[44] In effect, an ethnic security belt was stretched across northern Israel, and

58

FIGURE 5.4: LIMITED FORCES ZONE
OF 1949 GAA

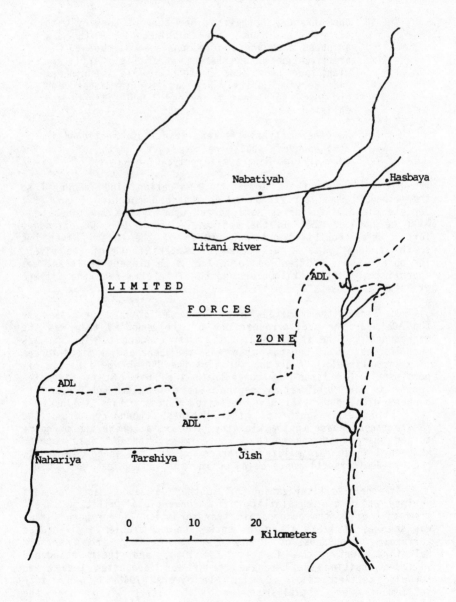

with a string of Zionist outposts facing Lebanon the Upper Galilee
would no longer offer unchallenged access for infiltrators and
raiders based in southern Lebanon. As Israel's Attorney General
stated in 1972, "we do not want Arab villages near the Lebanese
border. We do not want to provide an opportunity for them to
contact, or be contacted by Arabs on the other side." Arabs
expelled from the border villages of Ikrit and Berem in 1948 have
been refused access to their villages by the Israeli Government,
despite the fact that several of the villages' young men have
served loyally in the Israeli armed forces.[45]

In summary, therefore, the immediate military effect of the
GAA was to mollify Zionist fears about the defensibility of the
northern border. Lebanon, hardly a potent offensive threat in any
event, was prohibited from stationing more than 1,500 soldiers
south of a line running from the mouth of the Litani across to
Hasbaya. Although Israel was subject to parallel limitations,
there was nothing in the GAA preventing it from transforming its
side of the boundary into a series of fortified Jewish
settlements. The ethnic homogeneity of the frontier region was
destroyed, the fear of invasion from the north was diminished, and
the southern Lebanese battleground which had claimed many
Australian and Jewish lives in 1941 was almost completely
disarmed. Israel was not able to foresee in 1949 that a stronger
Lebanese presence south of the Litani would have helped facilitate
its own security. From the Israeli perspective of late March
1949, all that remained to be accomplished was the signing of a
peace treaty with Lebanon.

NOTES

1. Colonel Richard Meinertzhagen, Middle East Diary 1917-1965
(New York: Thomas Yoseloff, 1960), p. 64.

1. Stephen Hemsley Longrigg, Syria and Lebanon Under French
Mandate (London: Oxford University Press, 1958), p. 161.

3. Ibid.

4. Arnold J. Toynbee, ed., Survey of International Affairs 1925
(Volume I) (London: Oxford University Press, 1927), p. 433.

5. Ibid., p. 437.

6. Report of the Peel Commission as cited in Ibrahim Abu-Lughod,
ed., The Transformation of Palestine (Evanston: Northwestern
University Press, 1971), p. 298.

7. Times (London), 10 October 1938, p. 16.

60

8. _Times_ (London), 28 May 1938, p. 13.

9. Leonard Mosley, _Gideon Goes to War_ (New York: Charles Scribner's Sons, 1966), p. 57.

10. _Times_ (London), 2 May 1938, p. 15.

11. _Times_ (London), 28 May 1938, p. 13.

12. _Times_ (London), 26 July 1938, p. 11

13. _Times_ (London), 1 July 1938, p. 15.

14. _Times_ (London), 4 May 1939, p. 9.

15. See J. C. Hurewitz, _Diplomacy in the Near and Middle East, A Documentary Record: 1914-1956_, Volume II (Princeton: D. Van Nostrand Company, Inc., 1956), pp. 218-226.

16. Janet Abu-Lughod, "Demographic Transformation," in _The Transformation of Palestine_, p. 147.

17. John Ruedy, "Dynamics of Land Alienation," in _The Transformation of Palestine_, p. 121.

18. Janet Abu-Lughod, "Demographic Transformation," p. 153.

19. Hasan Sharif, "South Lebanon: Its History and Geo-politics," in _South Lebanon_, ed. Elaine Hagopian and Samih Farsoun (Detroit: Association of Arab-American University Graduates, 1978), p. 14.

20. Perhaps the most comprehensive account of Operation Exporter is to be found in Major General I. S. O. Playfair, _The Mediterranean and the Middle East_, Volume II (London: Her Majesty's Stationery Office, 1956). This work is part of the _History of the Second World War, United Kingdom Military Series_ ed. J. R. M. Butler.

21. Longrigg, _Syria and Lebanon Under French Mandate_, pp. 298, 309.

22. Ibid., p. 314.

23. According to Playfair, the 25th Infantry Brigade was still bottled up north of Jezzin when the French in Beirut capitulated. _The Mediterranean and the Middle East_, Volume II, p. 220.

24. Ibid., pp. 211-216.

25. Hurewitz, _Diplomacy in the Near and Middle East_, Volume II, p. 281.

26. "UN General Assembly Resolution 181 (II)," in Hurewitz, _Diplomacy in the Near and Middle East_, Volume II, pp. 289-292.

27. Edgar O'Ballance, The Arab-Israeli War, 1948 (London: Faber and Faber Limited, 1956), p. 185.

29. Lt. Colonel Netanel Lorch, The Edge of the Sword: Israel's War of Independence 1947-1949 (New York: G. P. Putnam's Sons, 1961), p. 155.

29. Harry Sacher, Israel: The Establishment of a State (New York: British Book Centre, 1952), pp. 233-234.

30. Lorch, The Edge of the Sword, pp. 155-156.

31. Ibid., p. 158.

32. O'Ballance, The Arab-Israel War, 1948, p. 113.

33. Lorch, The Edge of the Sword, p. 263.

34. Dan Kurzman, Genesis 1948 (Cleveland: The New American Library, Inc., 1970), p. 614.

35. Lorch, The Edge of the Sword, p. 378.

36. George Kirk, Survey of International Affairs: The Middle East 1945-1950 (London: Oxford University Press, 1954), pp. 288-289.

37. Quoted by Michael Bar-Zohar, Ben Gurion: The Armed Prophet (Englewood Cliffs, NJ: Prentice Hall, Inc., 1968), p. 130.

38. Times (London), 17 January 1949, p. 4.

39. Earl Berger, The Covenant and the Sword (London: Routledge and Kegan Paul Ltd., 1965), p. 30.

40. See John Norton Moore, ed., The Arab-Israeli Conflict. Volume III: Documents (Princeton: Princeton University Press, 1974), p. 392.

41. Ibid., p. 393.

42. Ibid.

43. State of Israel Yearbook 5712 (1951/52) (Jerusalem: Government Printer, October 1951), p. 269.

44. The following Jewish settlements were established either during or soon after the 1948 war: Rosh-Hanikra, Bar'am, Yiron, Malkiya, Yifta, Shelomi, and Qiryat Shemona. See Zev Vilnay, The New Israel Atlas, Bible to Present Day (Jerusalem: Israel Universities Press, 1968), pp. 109-112. For an account of Arabs

displaced from the border region within Israel, see Peter Grose, "Arabs Ejected from Homes in '48 May Not Return," <u>New York Times</u>, 24 July 1972, p. 2.

45. Grose, <u>New York Times</u>, 24 July 1972, p.2.

6. A Quiet Interlude: 1949–1967

Israel's hope of rapidly concluding a peace treaty with its northern neighbor proved illusory. In April 1949 the U.N. established a Conciliation Commission for Palestine which sponsored Arab-Israeli peace discussions at Lausanne, Switzerland. It was at Lausanne that Israel discovered that it had yielded its toehold on the Litani for nothing.

The Israeli proposal to Lebanon at Lausanne was stark in its simplicity but rich in its implications. Tel Aviv suggested that the ADL between the two countries be transformed by a treaty of peace into an official, internationally recognized boundary.[1] The new Jewish State was prepared to renounce the traditional Zionist claim to southern Lebanon in return for a simple declaration of peace, one which would imply (a) Lebanon's defection from an Arab world hostile to Israel; (b) a de facto alliance between the Jewish and Catholic minorities in the predominantly Muslim eastern Mediterranean coastal region; and (c) a cooperative, bilateral approach toward the exploitation of southern Lebanon's water resources.

The promise of an official Israeli acknowledgement of Beirut's sovereignty over southern Lebanon proved, however, to be an insufficient inducement. Lebanon made two counterproposals: first, that the 125,000 Palestinian Arabs who had fled to Lebanon from Palestine during the fighting of 1948 be repatriated by Israel; and second, that the portion of Western Galilee which had, in 1947, been set aside by the U.N. for the Arab sector of partitioned Palestine be turned over to Lebanon.[2] Presumably the refugees, 90 percent of whom were Muslims,[3] would be settled in that region, thus insuring that the narrow Christian majority in Lebanon proper would be preserved. Israel predictably rejected the Lebanese proposal, which if accepted would have expanded "southern Lebanon" to include Acre on the coast and Nazareth inland. The discussions ended with no agreement reached, and Lebanon settled into a policy of non-recognition of Israel.

Although it was obliged by the other Arab states and by a significant portion of its own citizenry to adhere to a tough negotiating line with the Israelis, Lebanon was quite sensitive to the military facts of life in the border region adjoining Israel. As was the case during the 1948 Arab-Israeli war, Beirut sought from 1949 on to enjoy the best of both worlds. Lebanon gave up the opportunity to obtain official Israeli recognition of its jurisdiction in southern Lebanon, but by so doing reaped a financial harvest from the Arab economic boycott of the Jewish State. Furthermore, it took substantive steps to ensure that Israel would have no reason or justification for the seizure of Lebanese territory. Diplomatic obduracy toward Israel was offset by a policy of cooperation in the frontier zone, a policy that sometimes bordered on obsequiousness.

Article VII of the GAA signed by Israel and Lebanon in March 1949 established an Israeli-Lebanese Mixed Armistice Commission (ILMAC) under U.N. auspices. ILMAC was authorized to establish two headquarters, one at the Israeli frontier post north of Metulla, and the other at the Lebanese frontier post at Ras an Naqurah. The mission of ILMAC was to enforce, on the basis of unanimous consent, the provisions of the GAA.[4] Both sides initially had good reasons for seeing ILMAC perform effectively. Lebanon wanted to avoid any and all acts of provocation that could bring about the reintroduction of Israeli forces to southern Lebanon. Israel desired Lebanese cooperation in preventing the return of Arab refugees while it consolidated a line of Jewish settlements along the boundary.

In November 1949, ILMAC faced its first difficult task. The Lebanese Government, claiming that raids were being conducted from Israel against its southern villages, requested that ILMAC clearly demarcate the ADL. The objective of the proposed boundary-marking exercise was to "put an end to frontier incidents," thereby presumably reducing the likelihood of an Israeli invasion.[5]

Prior to the Lebanese request the U.N. Conciliation Commission at Lausanne had indeed recommended that in cases where no competing territorial claims existed, Israel and its Arab neighbors should move toward the creation of recognized boundaries.[6] That suggestion had focused attention on the Lebanese-Israeli ADL, because notwithstanding the obvious interest of Zionism in southern Lebanon, there were no territorial disputes of a magnitude similar to those between Israel and Syria or Israel and Jordan. Lebanon rejected the idea of a formal boundary settlement, however, on the grounds that it would imply its recognition of the Jewish State. Still, Lebanon very badly wanted the ADL redemarcated. Every time a Lebanese villager strayed across the poorly marked boundary the Lebanese authorities feared an Israeli military response. Lebanon did not intend to give Israel any excuse to occupy Lebanese territory, but neither did it want to give the boundary international legal status through a peace treaty. Troubled by the border-crossing propensities of its own citizens, Lebanon apparently invented the pretext of Israeli raids in order to seize the initiative in requesting that the ADL be better defined on the ground.

Inasmuch as the original Anglo-French Boundary Commission had published a detailed report of its surveying procedures, it appeared that ILMAC's task was simple and straightforward: mark the ADL and post warning notices for the inhabitants of the frontier zone. Yet the 1923 boundary line bisected parcels of land in some places which were owned by single villages or individuals, a defect which had been successfully ameliorated by

the 1926 "good neighbourly relations" treaty. That accord, which
validated patterns of human interaction predating the existence of
Lebanon and Palestine, institutionalized cross-border movement in
the frontier region. The GAA of 1949, however, was a military
agreement undertaken by two hostile states, and as such it
authorized both sides to prohibit civilians from crossing the
ADL.[7]   Whereas the Jewish settlers occupying abandoned Arab
villages near the Lebanese border had no compelling reason or
desire to cross the ADL, Arab villagers in Lebanon were under the
impression that they could continue to graze cattle or plant
tobacco on "their" land, even though some of that land was now on
the "wrong" side of an all but invisible boundary. Since Israel
took sharp exception to Arab border crossings, Beirut concluded
that the requirement for absolute quiet in the frontier zone
outweighed the property rights and economic well-being of the
Lebanese villagers living next to Israel.

ILMAC established a special subcommittee on 16 November 1949
to study the 1923 boundary agreement and to post warning signs
along the ADL. The subcommittee completed its work on 27 January
1951,[8] leaving the boundary unfenced but well-marked except for
six kilometers "where the two sides maintained different
interpretations of the Franco-British frontier agreement of
1923."[9] Although some Jewish-owned land in southern Lebanon was
lost, the big losers were the Arab peasants of southern Lebanon.
Not only did they lose land, they were also denied access to jobs
and traditional markets on the Israeli side of the border. A
valuable economic safety valve had been lost, and ironically the
loss had been facilitated by official Lebanese initiative.

The boundary-marking project was supplemented by mixed
Israeli-Lebanese police investigations which were designed to stop
cross-border smuggling and theft. Many minor disputes involving
wandering livestock and fishing boats were expeditiously settled
by the mixed police, who operated under ILMAC auspices. Lebanese
police even assisted Israel in expelling to Lebanon several
hundred Arab refugees who had infiltrated into Israel for the
purpose of returning to their homes.[10]

According to Lieutenant-General Burns, Chief of Staff of the
U.N. Truce Supervision Organization (UNTSO) from August 1954 to
November 1956,

> UNTSO had very few difficulties in connexion with the
> General Armistice Agreement between Israel and Lebanon.
> In fact, the Israel-Lebanon MAC worked as it had been
> intended all MAC's should. It met at periodic intervals,
> and seldom had serious complaints to deal with. Those
> that were presented related mostly to grazing of cattle
> on the wrong side of the ADL.[11]

Burns did note, however, that the Lebanese were obliged to go out of their way to appease the Israelis in the border region. In 1955 some Israelis were killed by Arab infiltrators from Lebanon. The incident alarmed the Lebanese authorities, who set about quickly to remove "all refugees and people other than old established residents...from a zone ten kilometers deep on the Lebanese side of the border."[12]

By paying careful attention to Israeli sensitivities in the border area, Lebanon bought nearly two decades of peace with its southern neighbor. Yet its policy of local appeasement eventually came to naught. In the wake of the June 1967 Arab-Israeli war--a war which Lebanon characteristically avoided--Israel declared the 1949 armistice to be void. Furthermore, by the end of 1968 Israel began to hold Lebanon directly responsible for the activities of the armed Palestinians in the frontier region. After two decades of peace and prosperity, Lebanon found itself being drawn into the Arab-Israeli vortex.

Israel's stunning military successes of June 1967 left it in possession of the Sinai Peninsula, the balance of mandatory Palestine, and the Golan Heights. Its decision not to relinquish those territories to their former owners--Egypt, Jordan, and Syria--meant that the 1949 armistice agreements with those states no longer corresponded with de facto conditions. Three of the four armistice demarcation lines established in 1949 were, after the second week of June 1967, well to the rear of Israel's forward military positions. If the armistice agreements were still valid, Israel obviously would have been obliged to withdraw to positions behind the 1949 demarcation lines. However, Israel had no intention of making any such withdrawal, and instead took the position that "Arab aggression" in June 1967 had demolished the legal validity of the 1949 armistice accords. Furthermore, according to Israel, "The texts of the Agreements between Israel and Lebanon, Syria, Jordan and Egypt clearly point to the fact that the lines dividing them were of a provisional and non-political nature: they were not intended to, and did not constitute international boundaries."[13]

If the purported aggression of Egypt, Jordan, and Syria had provided Israel with justification for repudiating the 1949 armistice regime, what would its attitude be toward the GAA with Lebanon, its ostentatiously non-belligerent northern neighbor? According to General Odd Bull, Commander of UNTSO at the time of the 1967 war,

> There had been no hostilities between Israel and Lebanon during the June War, though Israeli planes were reported to have flown over Lebanese territory.... In spite of this Israel announced that its armistice agreement with Lebanon...was ended.[14]

According to Bull, Israel took the position that Lebanon had indeed been a legal participant in the conflict even though it had conducted no offensive military operations. During the war a junior Lebanese officer had refused an Israeli request for a meeting of ILMAC, stating that such a meeting was impossible because the two countries were at war.[15] That, claimed Israel, amounted to a declaration of war.

Furthermore, an article appeared in the New York Times in June 1967,[16] alleging that the Prime Minister of Lebanon had ordered the army to attack Israel, but that the army commander refused. The report implied that military insubordination alone had kept Lebanon from invading Israel. Inasmuch as the Lebanese Prime Minister lacks the authority to order the army into action, and in light of the report's additional claim that Lebanon had participated in the 1956 Arab-Israeli war (along with Syria), it may be concluded that the article was either misleading at best or irresponsible reporting at worst. Along with the "declaration of war" proclaimed by the Lebanese officer, the New York Times report clearly suggests that there was an interest in portraying Lebanon as being responsible for the destruction of the 1949 GAA.

The key question was whether or not Israel's scuttling of the GAA signaled a renewed effort to adjust the northern boundary and seize Lebanese water. The answer to that question appears to be a qualified "no." By failing to move into southern Lebanon during the June War itself, when an adequate pretext surely could have been invented, Israel demonstrated quite clearly that its repudiation of the armistice was not intended as a prelude to a new conquest. It appears instead that Israel's decision to terminate the GAA with Lebanon was prompted by a desire to take a legally and logically consistent position toward the entire Arab-Israeli armistice regime. Article VIII of the Israel-Lebanon GAA established procedures whereby the agreement could be modified "by mutual consent."[17] The other three Arab-Israeli armistice agreements contained similar language. None of the agreements provided for either bilateral or unilateral repudiation of any provision by any party, unless of course the GAAs were to be replaced by peace treaties. Israel's desire to hold Arab territories overrun in June 1967 forced it to take the position that all armistice agreements were dead. Israel could not very well adhere to the terms of the GAA with Lebanon while at the same time rejecting near-identical language appearing in the other three. It would have to repudiate all of the agreements or none. Furthermore, if it wished to base its repudiation of three of the agreements on a claim of Arab aggression in June 1967, then Israel would be obliged to find similar grounds on which to base its renunciation of the GAA with Lebanon. The purported Lebanese "declaration of war," supplemented by the questionable New York Times report, gave Israel the pretext to reject the GAA, thereby enabling it to take a consistent--if legally questionable-- position toward all of the armistice agreements. This conclusion

68

is supported by a March 1971 statement issued by the Israeli Ministry of Foreign Affairs on "The Provisional Nature of the 1949 Armistice Lines,"[18] a position paper that carefully mentioned Lebanon even though the objective of the statement was to provide the legal justification for the continued occupation of territories taken in June 1967. To uphold the Israel-Lebanon GAA would be to uphold the validity of the 1949 armistice demarcation lines with Egypt, Jordan, and Syria as well.

In addition to the breakdown of the GAA, the 1967 war extended the length of the Israeli-Lebanese border by about twelve miles, due to the advance of Israeli forces into the Golan Heights. Whereas the easternmost point of the common boundary had formerly been located just to the north of the Hula Valley, Lebanon now had to contend with the presence of Israel along the slopes of Mount Hermon to a point south of the village of Shab'a. The extension of the common boundary might have been of little or no significance had it not been for yet another consequence of the June War: the rise of fedayeen commando activity.

NOTES

1. Earl Berger, The Covenant and the Sword (London: Routledge and Kegan Paul Ltd., 1965), p. 55.

2. Ibid., p. 59.

3. Samir N. Saliba, The Jordan River Dispute (The Hague: Martinus Nijhoff, 1968), p. 80.

4. John Norton Moore, ed., The Arab-Israeli Conflict. Volume III: Documents (Princeton: Princeton University Press, 1974), pp. 394-395.

5. New York Times, 7 November 1949, p. 18.

6. Ibid.

7. Moore, Documents, p. 302.

8. Mohamad Taki Mehdi, "Arab-Israeli Tension: A Study of Border Conflicts." Unpublished thesis. University of California (Berkeley), 1953, p. 62.

9. Odd Bull, War and Peace in the Middle East (London: Leo Cooper, 1976), p. 62.

10. Mehdi, "Arab-Israeli Tension, A Study of Border Conflicts," p. 62.

11. Lieutenant General E. L. M. Burns, Between Arab and Israeli (London: George G. Harrap & Co., Ltd., 1962), p. 120.

12. Ibid., p. 122.

13. "The Provisional Nature of the 1949 Armistice Lines," Statement by the Israeli Ministry of Foreign Affairs, March 1971, in Crescent and Star: Arab & Israeli Perspectives on the Middle East Conflict, ed. Yonah Alexander and Nicholas N. Kittrie, p. 228.

14. Bull, War and Peace in the Middle East, p. 130.

15. Ibid., pp. 130-131.

16. New York Times, 21 June 1967, pp. 1, 18.

17. Moore, Documents, p. 395.

18. Alexander and Kittrie, Crescent and Star, pp. 218-219.

7. The Fedayeen Factor: 1968–1975

According to Edgar O'Ballance, the first fedayeen attack on Israel from Lebanon took place on 1 June 1965, when a small band of Palestinians slipped over the unguarded boundary and blew up a house in the hamlet of Yiftah.[1] It was not until October 1968, however, that the Palestinian commandos first entered Lebanon in significant numbers.

The defeat of the conventional Arab armies in June 1967 had left the growing Palestinian resistance movement as the only force willing to continue an armed struggle against Israel. Although the main fedayeen bases for armed operations were located in Jordan (prior to September 1970), commandos did begin to make their presence felt in southern Lebanon by late 1968. The official Lebanese reaction to the prospect of an organized fedayeen raiding campaign against Israel headquartered on Lebanese soil was predictably negative and fully in keeping with Beirut's desire to keep the frontier region totally quiet. According to Kamal Salibi,

> If the Lebanese authorities were willing to condone a limited amount of Palestinian military training on Lebanese territory, one thing which they were determined not to tolerate was Palestinian commando infiltration from Lebanon into Israel... While Israel argued that the former frontier between Palestine and Lebanon could only be regarded as an armistice line so long as Lebanon remained formally in a state of war with Israel, the Lebanese authorities were anxious not to give Israel any excuse to question this frontier and force even the least change in it.[2]

Three obstacles combined, however, to thwart Beirut's efforts at controlling Palestinian activities in the south. First was the small size of Lebanon's armed forces, which, by 1968, had reached a strength of approximately 13,200 men.[3] Such a small force would be hard-pressed to enforce discipline on the growing numbers of fedayeen in Lebanon, who were receiving financial and logistical support from other Arab states, particularly Syria. The second limitation on Beirut's ability to deal with the armed Palestinians was the skeletal government presence in southern Lebanon, a deficiency that allowed fedayeen forces relative freedom of movement. As Michael Hudson observed in early 1970,

> Often, the only evidence of Lebanese Government presence in South Lebanon's little hamlets is the shabby, one-room police post, with its faded flag hanging over the entrance. There are reports that guerrillas have been cordially received in these villages, despite the appalling danger they carry with them, because they minister to the medical and economic needs of the

villagers more effectively than the Lebanese Government
has been able to.[4]

The third, and by far the most significant obstacle preventing
Beirut from controlling the commandos, was Lebanon's chronic lack
of consensus on the question of national identity. Whereas most
of Lebanon's Muslim citizens and some Christians (especially
members of the Greek Orthodox sect) saw Lebanon as an Arab state
obligated to aid the Palestinian resistance movement, the Lebanese
economic and political elite--predominantly Maronite (but not
without Muslim Lebanese members)--viewed Lebanon as a halfway
house between East and West and urged that the country remain
aloof from the Arab-Israeli controversy. In April 1969 the Prime
Minister of Lebanon, Rashid Karami, summarized the government's
dilemma by stating that

> There are two sides in Lebanon, one saying commando
> action should be carried out from Lebanon whatever the
> circumstances, (and the other saying) the commandos
> represent a danger to Lebanon... That is why no
> government can take either view without splitting the
> country.[5]

The official Israeli policy toward the _fedayeen_ presence in
Lebanon was first enunciated _before_ cross-border operations from
Lebanon had begun in earnest. An attack on an Israeli civilian
airliner at the Athens airport on 26 December 1968 by two Arabs
from Lebanon prompted Israel's Transport Minister, Moshe Carmel,
to state that Israel would not "relieve the Government of Lebanon
from responsibility for acts of sabotage organized on Lebanese
soil with governmental encouragement."[6] Two days later, on 23
December 1968, Israeli commandos raided the Beirut International
Airport and destroyed thirteen civilian planes. Unlike their
British predecessors thirty years earlier, the Israelis chose not
to inquire politely about the possibility of Lebanese assistance
in controlling the activities of anti-Zionist Arabs.

During the early part of 1969, _fedayeen_ activity in Lebanon
consisted almost exclusively of establishing base camps in the
foothills of Mount Hermon (the Arqub) and securing supply trails
into the Arqub from Syria. Later the area would become known as
"Fatahland," after _al-Fatah_, the largest and most active of the
many autonomous _fedayeen_ organizations. Gradually the Lebanese
Government disappeared from the Arqub, and the Lebanese Army took
up positions on the west bank of the Hasbani River to prevent the
Palestinians from establishing bases near the old Palestine-
Lebanon boundary. Commando activity emanating from Lebanon was
therefore limited for the most part to raids on Israeli targets in
the occupied Golan Heights. In the spring of 1969, however, the
fedayeen began to probe along the Hasbani River, thereby provoking
clashes with the Lebanese Army. The first major encounter
occurred on 14 April 1969, when the Army evicted armed
Palestinians from the village of Dayr Mimass.[7] Open warfare raged
during the autumn of 1969 as the Lebanese Army attempted, with

some success, to bottle up the fedayeen east of the Hasbani and restrict the flow of men and supplies to the Arqub from Syria. On 3 December 1969 the fighting ended, and an accord known as the "Cairo Agreement" was signed. Designed to govern Lebanese-Palestinian relations, the Cairo Agreement divided southern Lebanon into three regions. In the Arqub, or eastern sector, the fedayeen were granted virtual autonomy. In the central sector of the Israel-Lebanon border region, responsibility for military defense was left with the Lebanese Army, but a fedayeen presence in limited numbers and in specified locations was permitted. In the western sector, or coastal plain, no armed Palestinians would be allowed outside of refugee camps.[8]

In reality the Cairo Agreement settled nothing. Fedayeen raids into the occupied Golan Heights continued and Israeli retaliation against Lebanese territory predictably followed. The Lebanese Government was caught squarely in the middle. Michael Hudson expressed the triangular relationship as follows:

> Victory for the Lebanese Government was in proportion to its ability to seal off the commandos from Israeli territory and avert Israeli reprisals, but for the commandos such an outcome would mean defeat. Lebanon's gains would be the Palestinians' losses. But enhanced commando access to Israel meant certain retaliation: commando gains would be Lebanese losses. As a third party to the conflict, it was to Israel's interest to hinder any modus vivendi between the two by keeping up the pressure on the Lebanese.[9]

Pressure was indeed applied. On 6 March 1970 the Israeli Northern District Commander, Major General Mordechai Gur, reportedly threatened to "turn a six-mile stretch of southern Lebanon into a scorched-earth desert."[10] Fifteen years earlier the Lebanese Government had felt constrained to remove all Palestinian refugees from that same six mile (ten kilometer) strip. In May 1970 a thirty-two-hour sweep of the Arqub was conducted by an Israeli force of about 2,000 men. Another sweep of the Arqub took place between 25 and 28 February 1972 following a warning by Israeli Chief of Staff Lieutenant General David Elazar that fedayeen activity was "liable to bring disaster upon the villages of south Lebanon."[11] After the Arqub operation Defense Minister Moshe Dayan announced that Israel reserved the right to occupy Lebanese territory indefinitely unless Beirut took steps to oust the commandos from the slopes of Mount Hermon.[12] Another Israeli sweep--this time through the Marj Valley and along the Mediterranean coast--took place on 16 and 17 September 1972 following the murders of Israeli athletes at the Munich Olympic Games.

Following the September 1972 operation the commandos acceded to new territorial restrictions imposed by the Lebanese Government. However, on 15 October 1972, Israel launched air attacks against Palestinian bases in Lebanon and announced that it would no longer wait for commando acts or terrorist incidents before striking targets in Lebanon. Former Israeli Chief of Staff Chaim Herzog announced that "We are not engaged in reprisal, but a war against terror. The very presence of terrorists in the area between the border and the Litani River is a provocation, and Israel is free to act against them."[13]

According to Lebanese Government sources there were forty-four major Israeli attacks on Lebanon between mid-1968 and mid-1974, resulting in the deaths of 880 Lebanese and Palestinian civilians.[14] As Hudson has observed,

> That these attacks were a major drain on Lebanon's thin governmental legitimacy is self evident. It is also manifest that the traditional Maronite leaders and their constituencies had come to regard the Palestinian guerrillas, rather than Israel itself, as chiefly to blame for this state of affairs.[15]

Prior to 1971 the main fedayeen bases for operations against Israel were located in northwestern Jordan.[16] The camps in the Arqub of Lebanon were strictly subsidiary. Yet the Jordanian civil war of September 1970 and subsequent mopping-up operations by the Jordan Arab Army in the Spring of 1971 caused the focus of fedayeen activity to shift to "Fatahland," the result being a fundamental shift of Israeli anti-fedayeen activities from Jordan to Lebanon. According to O'Ballance, some 9,000 fedayeen escaped from Jordan to Syria in 1971, and by November of the same year the commando buildup began in the Arqub. Nevertheless,

> Raids from the Lebanon Arqub region into Israel had been limited in scope as the Israelis were in good positions in the overlooking hills, and in fact had constructed a road to supply them, a mile or so of which actually lay within Lebanese territory.[17]

In summary, fedayeen activity in southern Lebanon between the third and fourth Arab-Israeli wars was not particularly effective and had a very limited impact on northern Israel. The commandos were, for the most part, restricted to the Arqub region of Lebanon. With a few minor exceptions their cross-border activities were limited to the occupied Golan Heights and had little effect on Israeli settlements lying astride the 1949 GAA. It is worth noting that it was not until May 1974 that Israel began to build a barrier--a latter-day version of Tegart's Wall--along the old Palestine-Lebanon boundary.[18] Between the autumn of 1968, when fedayeen in noticeable numbers began to arrive in southern Lebanon, and July 1974, the border between Lebanon and Israel contained no significant physical obstacle.[19]

Israel's policy of striking at Palestinian targets in Lebanon was not, therefore, the result of a commando campaign in the Acre and Safed subdistricts, as had been the case in 1938. To the extent that Israeli attacks on Lebanon were retaliatory in nature,

they stemmed from acts of international terrorism against Israelis
and from commando activity in the occupied Golan Heights. To the
extent that the attacks were not retaliatory--as indicated by
Herzog's statement cited above--Israel's main interest seemed to
lie in provoking a violent confrontation between Lebanon's
Maronite community and the Palestinian commandos. Following a
bold Israeli commando raid on Beirut on 10 April 1973, which
resulted in the deaths of three Palestinian leaders, fighting
broke out between the Lebanese Army and the fedayeen which lasted
from 1-17 May. According to Hudson the fighting, which took place
mainly in the vicinity of the Palestinian refugee camps of Beirut,
"led only to a standoff" and was a "psychological defeat for the
Army."[20]

In the Spring of 1974 the Palestinian-Israeli confrontation
acquired a new dimension, as fedayeen raiders from southern
Lebanon began to strike into Israel proper. On 11 April 1974
three commandos stormed an apartment building in the Israeli town
of Qiryat Shemona, ultimately killing sixteen Israeli civilians
and two soldiers. On the next day Israeli forces retaliated by
blowing up buildings in five Lebanese border villages. Defense
Minister Dayan called upon Lebanon to eliminate the commando
presence, adding ominously, "The Lebanese villagers will have to
abandon their homes and flee if the people of Qiryat Shemona
cannot live in peace. All of southern Lebanon will not be able to
exist."[21] The U.N. Security Council condemned the Israeli raids,
prompting Israel's delegate to state that Israel would "continue
to hold the Lebanese Government responsible for any armed attacks
organized in or perpetrated from Lebanon."[22]

On 15 May 1974 three fedayeen commandos raided the Israeli
border village of Maalot, killing twenty-five Israelis. Israel
refrained from a ground attack against Lebanon, but bombing raids
against Palestinian targets in Lebanon produced heavy
casualties.[23] On 13 June 1974 a fedayeen attack on the Israeli
settlement of Shamir resulted in the deaths of three women and
brought more Israeli air attacks on Lebanon.[24] A seaborne raid on
the Israeli town of Nahariya on 24 June 1974 produced four Israeli
deaths and brought Palestinian positions in southern Lebanon under
heavy Israeli artillery attacks. Later, Israeli gunboats shelled
three Lebanese ports in further retaliation for the Nahariya
operation.[25]

Shortly after the raid on Qiryat Shemona, Israel decided to
try to seal the Lebanese boundary with a twelve-foot high security
fence topped with barbed wire and equipped with electronic warning
devices. A smooth dirt track was created on the Israeli side of
the fence to pick up footprints, and machinegun positions were
established at intervals along the fence. The security barrier
proved to be far more effective than its 1938 predecessor because
of the absence of Arabs (except for loyal Israeli Druze) on the
Israeli side of the border. Yet the new security system was not
infallible. As one Israeli officer observed,

> We realize it's impossible to seal the border completely.
> But this fence will at least slow a terrorist down. If
> the system works properly, we'll be able to kill him
> before he manages to cut his way through.[26]

Indeed, the largest number of commandos who participated in any of
the bloody raids that terrorized northern Israel in 1974 was only
four. Even with an elaborate security system it would be no easy
task to stop small groups of infiltrators, particularly if they
were willing (if not eager) to sacrifice their lives.

It is clear that the sudden rash of assaults on Israeli
civilians dramatically increased popular pressure on the Israeli
Government to "do something" about the fedayeen presence in
southern Lebanon. Civil war in Lebanon--a conflict brought on in
large measure by the seemingly endless cycle of Palestinian-
Israeli violence in the border region--afforded Israel the
opportunity to "do something" far more effective than conducting
retaliatory raids and building security fences. The total
collapse of Lebanon's weak central authority enabled Israel to
enlist the aid of anti-fedayeen Lebanese militiamen in the defense
of northern Israel.

NOTES

1. Edgar O'Ballance, Arab Guerrilla Power 1967-72 (Hamden:
Anchor Books, 1974), p. 30.

2. Kamal S. Salibi, Crossroads to Civil War: Lebanon 1958-1976
(Delmar, NY: Caravan Books, 1976), p. 27.

3. Area Handbook for Lebanon (Washington: U.S. Government
Printing Office, 1974), p. 297.

4. Michael Hudson, "Fedayeen are Forcing Lebanon's Hand," Mid
East, Volume X, Number 1, February 1970, p. 13.

5. Lester A. Sobel, ed., Palestinian Impasse: Arab Guerrillas &
International Terror (New York: Facts on File, Inc., 1977), p.
66.

6. Ibid., p. 36.

7. Michael Hudson, "The Palestinian Factor in the Lebanese Civil
War," Middle East Journal, Volume 32, No. 3, Summer 1978, p. 263.

8. Sharif, "South Lebanon: Its History and Geopolitics," in
South Lebanon, ed. Elaine Hagopian and Samih Farsoun (Detroit:
Association of Arab-American University Graduates, 1978), p. 16.

9. Hudson, "Fedayeen Are Forcing Lebanon's Hand", p. 14.

10. Sobel, Palestinian Impasse, p. 91.

11. Ibid., p. 139

12. Ibid., p. 141

13. Ibid., p. 144.

14. Hudson, "The Palestinian Factor in the Lebanese Civil War," p. 263.

15. Ibid.

16. John K. Cooley, Green March, Black September (London: Frank Cass, 1973), p. 103.

17. O'Ballance, Arab Guerrilla Power, p. 122.

18. Terence Smith, "Israel Builds New Border Fence," New York Times, 14 July 1974, pp. 1, 17.

19. "For the most of its length the border is marked by neither fences nor mine fields. It takes little bravado to stroll a few yards into Lebanon, and people do so." Charles Mohr, "Lebanese Border with Israel Calm," New York Times, 7 November 1969, p. 5.

20. Hudson, "The Palestinian Factor in the Lebanese Civil War," p. 266.

21. Sobel, Palestinian Impasse, p. 209.

22. Ibid.

23. Ibid., p. 210.

24. Ibid., p. 212.

25. Ibid., pp. 213-214.

26. Smith, "Israel Builds New Border Fence," p. 1.

8. Civil War and the South: 1975-1978

Between April 1975 and October 1976 Lebanon was convulsed in a civil war that resulted in widespread physical destruction, the collapse of the country's fragile political system, and over 40,000 deaths, most of which were innocent civilians. The war began as a confrontation between the Maronite militias, eager to restrict or eliminate the troublesome Palestinian presence in Lebanon, and the fedayeen. In short order, however, Lebanese dissidents nursing old grudges against the country's political and economic elite entered the fight, transforming the Maronite-Palestinian clashes into a true civil war. Syria intervened twice in Lebanon on the side of the fedayeen and their Lebanese allies, successfully overcoming the Christian militias. Shortly thereafter, however, the war again erupted, as the pro-Palestinian Lebanese National Movement rejected the mildly reformist Syrian political formula for peace.[1] That rejection caused an unbelievable turnabout in the Syrian position. As James Markham put it,

> Most dramatically, at the height of the Lebanese civil war in the summer of 1976, Syrian armor lunged deep into Lebanon and clashed with the Palestinians, who seemed on the verge of victory over Christian rightists that might have provoked what Mr. Assad the President of Syria feared most--an untimely war with Israel.[2]

The Syrian military campaign, conducted in concert with the Christian militias, eventually overcame the Palestinian resistance, and a shaky peace was restored to Lebanon, except for the south. On 14 April 1976 Israeli Prime Minister Rabin, anticipating further Syrian armed intervention in Lebanon, announced the existence of an unspecified "red line" in Lebanon, south of which Syrian forces would not be permitted to move.[3] Although it was widely assumed that the "red line" was the lower course of the Litani River, subsequent developments suggested that it may have been the limited-forces line of the 1949 GAA. It will be recalled that the line extended from the mouth of the Litani, through Nabatiyah, to Hasbaya. When in January 1977 a Syrian battalion occupied Nabatiyah (north of the Litani), vigorous Israeli complaints led to its withdrawal.[4]

The Lebanese civil war had induced most of the fedayeen commandos stationed near the Israeli border to move north in order to fight the Christian militias and the Syrians. The Rabin government viewed the Palestinian evacuation as an opportunity to solve once and for all the vexatious problem of border security. It therefore became Israel's goal to bar the reintroduction of fedayeen commandos to the frontier region. The lessons of the past clearly indicated to Israel that the pacification of southern Lebanon was the prerequisite for the security of its own northern settlements.

The new Israeli policy, as announced by Defense Minister Shimon Peres on 19 July 1976, was what Peres called the "good fence program."[5] There were three aspects of the program: humanitarian relief for the beleaguered residents of southern Lebanese border villages; the exclusion of all non-Lebanese military forces from the area adjoining Israel; and the creation of a pro-Israeli southern Lebanese militia to aid in barring the reintroduction of fedayeen commandos. Although Israelis, when referring to the "good fence program," stress its humanitarian aspect, it is more accurate to view the entire undertaking in the context of a comprehensive security policy.

The humanitarian element of the program amounted to a series of Israeli gestures designed to establish a bond of friendship between the Lebanese civilians of the border region and the government of Israel.[6] The security fence which had divided Lebanon and Israel since 1974 was opened at two places: Metulla and Dovev. By providing to Lebanese citizens (most of whom--due to the location of the fence openings--were Maronite Christians) such vital services as water, medical care, employment, markets for agricultural produce, and access to Israeli-manufactured goods, Israel hoped to turn the residents of the Lebanese border villages into willing collaborators against the fedayeen.

The second element of the "good fence program" was the attempt to exclude non-Lebanese (Syrian and Palestinian) military forces from the south. Rabin's "red line" statement of 14 April 1976 was later supplemented by Foreign Minister Allon's proposal of 31 January 1977 that a multilateral agreement be reached concerning the presence of Arab military units near the Israeli-Lebanese border.[7] Allon reiterated his proposal on 13 February 1977, emphasizing that Israel would accept the stationing only of Lebanese forces in the frontier zone.[8] Israel was obviously opposed to the reintroduction of fedayeen commandos and was likewise opposed to the idea of Syrian regulars directly facing Israel on a new front.

The third element of the security program involved an attempt to fill the security vacuum which Israel and the virtually nonexistent Lebanese central authority had created in southern Lebanon. The Lebanese Army, reflecting the same contradictions that had brought Lebanon itself to ruin in 1975 and 1976, had all but collapsed. It was simply not prepared to move south in 1976. In order to obstruct the return of the Palestinians, therefore, Israel was faced with the choice of either occupying southern Lebanon or creating and supporting a pro-Israeli Arab force to police the area. Beginning in August 1976 Israel greatly increased the frequency of armored patrols penetrating several miles into Lebanon in order to check for fedayeen concentrations.[9] By October of the same year, however, much of the patrolling activity in Lebanon was being carried out by a pro-Israeli militia led by Major Saad Haddad, a Christian officer of the recently disintegrated Lebanese Army. Armed, clothed, fed, and trained by Israel, the militia's mission was to give northern Israel an "early-warning system, permitting it the IDF to move a task force into Lebanon quickly" should the Lebanese militia encounter Palestinian commandos.[10] Although many of the militiamen were locals who, like their kinsmen in 1925, had no great love for non-Christian Arabs, some were reportedly transported by Israel to southern Lebanon from Juniyah (the Maronite "capital" north of Beirut) by way of Haifa.[11] Haddad's strange role in the southern Lebanese political vacuum was demonstrated by the fact that as leader of the 3,000-man militia,[12] he (1) collaborated fully with Israel, (2) received orders from and reported directly to Maronite political and military leaders in Beirut,[13] and (3) continued to receive his regular pay from the official Lebanese Government of President Sarkis,[14] whose desires he routinely ignored and obstructed.

So long as _fedayeen_ forces in Lebanon found themselves fighting Syrians, the "good fence program" worked relatively well for Israel. Yet the Syrian-imposed peace in Lebanon in the autumn of 1976 permitted large numbers of armed Palestinians to again move south and join their Lebanese allies still active in the Shi'a villages of southern Lebanon. Syria, angered and embarrassed by the open collaboration of certain of its Maronite "allies" with Israel, again changed direction and facilitated the reentry of armed Palestinians to the south of Lebanon. The Syrian objective was not to help reinstitute _fedayeen_ attacks on Israel, but to punish those elements of the Maronite community who had welcomed Syrian intervention in June 1976 only to seriously humiliate the Assad regime (itself based on a religious minority group)[15] by blatant cooperation with the Israeli military. Inasmuch as Syria could not move its own forces south of the "red line" without provoking an Israeli military response, the only alternative was to turn the Palestinians loose on Major Haddad's militia.

Severe fighting broke out in southern Lebanon in February 1977, as Haddad's rightist militia attacked Palestinian and Lebanese leftist positions in the villages of Kafr Tibnit and Ibil as Saqy,[16] north of Israel's Hula Valley. Attacks and counterattacks continued through July 1977, with Israel providing artillery and logistical support to its Arab allies in an effort to create an anti-_fedayeen_ buffer zone along the entire length of the Israeli-Lebanese boundary. Syria gave parallel support to the Palestinian-leftist forces. Israeli support for the Maronite militia in the south became more open and militant with the coming to power of Prime Minister Menachem Begin in June 1977. On 8 August Begin publicly called attention to Israel's support of the militia, claiming that the _fedayeen_ had embarked on a program of "genocide" against the Christians of southern Lebanon. By affirming that Israel would "never abandon the Christian minority across the border,"[17] Begin was clearly raising the stakes in Lebanon. No longer was Israel engaged in a tactical campaign aimed simply at providing adequate frontier security. Begin's open proclamation of support for the Christians appeared to signal Israel's interest in, if not open support of, the idea of

splitting Lebanon itself along sectarian lines, with the
predominantly Christian areas of Mount Lebanon and east Beirut
linked to its Jewish neighbor to the south by a neutralized
southern Lebanon. As one observer noted,

> some sections of the Lebanese right wing have been so
> encouraged by the Israeli premier's recent public
> statement of support for their cause that they have been
> echoing Israeli calls for an international buffer force
> to be deployed in south Lebanon.[18]

On 19 July 1977 Palestinian forces agreed to stop fighting in
southern Lebanon.[19]   On the next day delegations representing the
Palestinians, the Syrian Army, the Lebanese Army, and the Arab
Deterrent Forces (then a predominantly Syrian peacekeeping force
in Lebanon authorized by the Arab League) met at Shtawra, Lebanon,
to map out a common strategy. An agreement was reached on 25
July. The Shtawra Agreement provided that fedayeen commandos
would withdraw to a line roughly fifteen kilometers from the
Israeli-Lebanese border, and that the reconstituted Lebanese Army
would move south and relieve the pro-Israeli Haddad militia of its
border-security functions.[20]

The United States moved quickly to capitalize on the Shtawra
Agreement by pressing for Israeli cooperation. On 11 September
the New York Times reported Lebanese press sources as stating that
Israel had informed the US that it "would not object" to the
presence of the Lebanese Army along the boundary provided that the
promised Palestinian withdrawal were effected, and that the
Palestinians agreed to conduct no more cross-border operations.[21]
It appeared that an agreement was within reach, and that Lebanon
was ready to deploy approximately two-thirds of its 3,000-man
rebuilt army to the south.[22]

Despite its promising start, the Shtawra Agreement foundered
on the all-important matter of timing and was never implemented.
President Sarkis was extremely reluctant to deploy his new army to
the south without first assuring himself that the pacification
plan would work. He did not want the Army, a key institution in
the rebuilding of Lebanon, to be subjected again to divisive
forces. Yet the question of who exactly would make the first move
in the pacification of southern Lebanon became the major stumbling
block. The Palestinian forces made their withdrawal contingent
upon the insertion of the regular Lebanese Army in the border
area. Sarkis, however, refused to deploy the Army without
assurances from the US that Israel would not undermine the
operation. Israel refused to give such assurances without first
seeing a total Palestinian withdrawal.[23] In an atmosphere of
mutual distrust the fighting in the south resumed. Clashes in the
vicinity of Marj 'Uyun and Al Khiyam, just north of Metulla, again
brought Israeli forces into Lebanese territory in support of their
militia allies.[24]

The US refused, however, to allow the Shtawra initiative to die and on 26 September 1977 arranged a ceasefire in southern Lebanon. Under the ceasefire formula, the entrance of the Lebanese Army and withdrawal of <u>fedayeen</u> units would take place simultaneously in early October. Israeli forces immediately withdrew from Lebanon.[25] However, the ceasefire was vigorously opposed by Major Haddad, who made the following statement:

> The cease-fire was forced on us... No one asked us. Others obligated us. We were against it. We are not against peace, but this cease-fire is not fair.

> They should have provided for a concurrent withdrawal by the Israeli Army and the guerrillas. That's the way we thought a cease-fire should be. I cannot understand how Israel accepted a condition like this, specifying a one-sided troop pullback, even if it was imposed by the United States.[26]

Within three weeks the ceasefire had broken down. Despite the Israeli withdrawal from southern Lebanon and the initiation of direct talks between Israeli and Lebanese officers in early October,[27] the Haddad militia and Palestinians simply could not refrain from sniping at one another. Haddad's forces in southern Lebanon urged their Israeli supporters to scrap the ceasefire, and the Israeli Defense Minister obliged them by making the implementation of the ceasefire contingent upon a unilateral Palestinian withdrawal from Al Khiyam, only five kilometers north of Metulla.[28] The Palestinians refused, fighting resumed, and again Sarkis declined to insert his army into the southern Lebanese maelstrom. Adding to the general confusion were demands by Israel that Lebanon recognize Major Haddad's militia as part of the regular Lebanese Army, and that Israel be permitted to maintain its "good fence" relationship with Lebanese border villages for an indefinite period.[29] Despite the fact that Haddad remained on the Lebanese Government payroll, the Syrian-supported Sarkis regime was in no position to accept the Israeli demands.

The ceasefire was finally killed on 8 November 1977, when <u>fedayeen</u> forces, firmly in control of the coastal sector of southern Lebanon, rocketed the Israeli town of Nahariya for the second time in three days, killing three Israelis. Israel retaliated by bombing Ar Rashidiyah refugee camp, killing about seventy people.[30] Sporadic fighting continued in the south, with Israeli forces occasionally crossing the border to assist Haddad's militia.

By March 1978, however, it was clear that Israel's attempt to establish an anti-<u>fedayeen</u> security zone on Lebanese territory along the length of the boundary had met with only partial success. Although the combination of Israeli patrolling and Haddad's militia activity had reduced Palestinian actions against Israel to infrequent and ineffective indirect fire attacks, the fact remained that long stretches of the boundary were still vulnerable. According to a map appearing in the Israeli press, only three small Christian enclaves existed on the Lebanese side of the border, and it was only in those areas where Israel could rely upon its allies to provide effective security.[31] Despite the sound civic action principles embodied in the "good fence program," Israel apparently succeeded in securing the cooperation of only 20,000 Lebanese living in the Christian border enclaves.[32] By supporting Major Haddad's militia Israel was in danger of forfeiting the cooperation of the Shi'a in southern Lebanon. This was recognized by an Israeli journalist, who observed that

> Without forsaking its alliance with the Christians and without leaving the Christian militias to their fate, Israel must now show initiative and imagination and pave a way to the heart of the Moslem population residing right next to it. Precisely because the Shi'ites are a minority within the Sunni Moslem world encircling us, they will need the defense of those same elements who had shown their loyalty to other minorities in the Middle East.[33]

In February 1978, the Israeli military reportedly made a serious effort to establish such links with the Shi'a community in the frontier zone. According to the Shi'a spiritual leader, Mufti Abdel Amir Kabalan, Israeli forces occupied the Shi'a village of Mays al Jabal in early February and offered the town's residents the entire "good fence" package in return for cooperation against the Palestinians. The villagers politely refused, pointing out that no fedayeen were based in Mays al Jabal. According to the Mufti, the Israeli overtures were rejected in six other Shi'a border villages.[34]

By basing its security policy on the small Christian minority of southern Lebanon, Israel found itself on shaky ground in the highly charged atmosphere of sectarian and village rivalries in the Jabal 'Amil region. Unless it could build bridges to the Shi'a community of the south, Israel would be obligated to constantly intervene in those parts of the border region beyond Haddad's control. On 11 March 1978, however, a terrorist atrocity in Israel gave the Begin government an opportunity to create new facts for southern Lebanon, the most important of which included a significant expansion of Major Haddad's territory and constituency.

NOTES

1. The Syrian-backed program, known for a time as the "New Lebanese National Covenant," is summarized by Kamal S. Salibi, Crossroads to Civil War: Lebanon 1958-1976 (Delmar: Caravan Books, 1976), pp. 163-164.

2. James M. Markham, "Syria's Role in Lebanon is Murkier than Ever," New York Times, 26 March 1978, p. 2E.

3. New York Times, 15 April 1976, p. 4.

4. Ibid., 26 January 1977, p. 2, and 13 February 1977, p. 5.

5. Ibid., 20 July 1976, p. 3.

6. An account of the humanitarian side of the "good fence program" was written by Gertrude Samuels, "Israel's New Experiment in Peace," New Leader, 27 September 1976, pp. 9-11.

7. New York Times, 1 February 1977, p. 5.

8. Ibid., 14 February 1977, p. 5.

9. Terence Smith, "Israelis Stepping up Patrols in Lebanon." New York Times, 3 August 1976, pp. 1, 4.

10. Henry Tanner, "In South Lebanon, an Odd War: Arab Soldiers with Israeli Arms," New York Times, 8 October 1976, pp. 1, 7.

11. Ibid., p. 7.

12. Jay Bushinsky, "Lebanese Major Shows Israelis His Touchy Position," Christian Science Monitor, 14 October 1977, p. 10.

13. Le Figaro (Paris), 20 April 1978, p. 16 (Foreign Broadcast Information Sevice, 24 April 1978, p. G4).

14. Bushinsky, "Lebanese Major Shows Israelis His Touchy Position," p. 10.

15. As a member of the minority Alawite sect, Assad's position in predominantly Sunni Syria was jeopardized by his "rescue" of the Lebanese Maronite elite. See "Syria Has an Enemy Within," New York Times, 4 Sept. 1977, Sect. 4, p. 2.

16. Keesing's Contemporary Archives, 23 December 1977, p. 28734.

17. Ibid.

18. Helena Cobban, "Pacifying South Lebanon Tied to Israeli Cooperation" Christian Science Monitor, 19 August 1977, p. 4.

19. Keesing's Contemporary Archives, 23 December 1977, p. 28736.

20. Ibid.

21. New York Times, 11 September 1977, p. 14.

22. Ibid.

86

23. <u>Keesing's Contemporary Archives</u>, 23 December 1977, p. 28736.

24. Ibid.

25. Ibid., p. 28737.

26. Bushinsky, "Lebanese Major Shows Israelis His Touchy Position," p. 10.

27. <u>New York Times</u>, 29 October 1977, p. 5.

28. Jason Morris, "Shaky Truce Invites Israeli Troops Again," <u>Christian Science Monitor</u>, 17 October 1977, p. 7.

29. Helena Cobban, "S. Lebanon: Integration with Israel?" <u>Christian Science Monitor</u>, 9 November 1977, p. 34.

30. Geoffrey Godsell, "Israeli Retaliation Raids Buffet U.S. Peace Efforts," <u>Christian Science Monitor</u>, 10 November 1977, pp. 1, 11.

31. <u>Jerusalem Post</u> (International Edition), 21 March 1978, p. 7.

32. Cobban, "S. Lebanon: Integration with Israel?" p. 34.

33. Shemu'el Segev, <u>Tel Aviv Ha'arez</u>, 12 April 1978, p. 5 (Foreign Broadcast Information Service, 13 April 1978, p. N5).

34. Marvine Howe, "Israelis Said to be Seeking Use of Lebanese Villages," <u>New York Times</u>, 26 February 1978, p. 11.

9. The March 1978 Invasion and Aftermath

On 11 March 1978 Palestinian commandos seized an Israeli bus near Tel Aviv in an action which resulted in thirty-seven deaths.[1] Although the entire world recognized the inevitability of an Israeli reprisal against Lebanon, the scope and intensity of the Israeli operation came as a great surprise.

In retrospect it appears that the Palestinian action of 11 March was not the cause of Israel's subsequent invasion. Rather it provided the Begin government with a strong public-relations basis upon which an already urgently needed military operation could be launched. The salient feature of the military situation in southern Lebanon in the beginning of March 1978 was the conspicuous failure of Major Haddad's militia to extend its control beyond the three Christian border enclaves. The very size of the Israeli invasion on 15 March suggests that it was a well-planned action designed to clear fedayeen and Lebanese leftist forces from the frontier region, not a spontaneous reaction to a particularly gruesome incident of Palestinian terrorism.

On 2 March 1978 Haddad's militia made a strong effort to break out of a Christian enclave. It seized the small village of Marun ar Ra's, [2] located only slightly more than one kilometer from the Israeli border. The significance of Marun ar Ra's lay, however, not in its proximity to Israel, but in its elevated position overlooking the town of Bint Jubayl two kilometers to the northwest. As was the case forty years earlier when Arab guerrillas were raising havoc along the Palestine-Lebanon border, Bint Jubayl was, in March 1978, the major commando stronghold in the central sector of the boundary region. Despite the many changes wrought over six decades, Bint Jubayl still enjoyed some significance as a road junction in the Lebanese portion of the divided Upper Galilee.

The Palestinians and their Lebanese allies counterattacked immediately and expelled Haddad's militia from Marun ar Ra's.[3] The engagement, though hardly a candidate for inclusion in a list of the world's great battles, nevertheless demonstrated conclusively to Israel that Haddad would not be able on his own to crack the enemy stronghold in and around Bint Jubayl. In order to sweep the fedayeen and their Lebanese partners from the Shi'a border villages, Israeli regulars would have to be used.

At 1:40 a.m. on 15 March 1978, Israeli artillery opened up on Lebanese villages held by the Palestinians and leftists.[4] The shelling was followed by a ground attack, with approximately 20,000 Israeli soldiers advancing on five axes.[5] In only two places, Bint Jubayl and At Tayibah, did the Palestinian-leftist coalition offer significant resistance.[6] The overwhelming majority of commandos simply evacuated their positions and headed north.

Although Israel had obviously contemplated a large incursion
into Lebanon prior to the Palestinian terrorist action of 11
March, it appears that military events which unfolded after 15
March involved a good deal of politically inspired improvisation.
At first the objective was limited: "to break the tightening
terrorist stranglehold around the Christian enclaves in the
central and northern sectors of southern Lebanon."[7]   In other
words, the Israeli operation--code-named "Stone of Wisdom"--was
designed to save Major Haddad's crumbling position.   Indeed,
Haddad greeted the invasion with undisguised relief, saying "I've
been waiting for this night a long time."[8] So had his men. As
the Israeli forces moved north, Haddad's militia followed in their
wake, looting the Shi'a villages which had successfully held out
for so long.[9]

The military objective was achieved within approximately
fifteen hours. The significance of the operation was explained as
follows by the Israeli Chief of Staff:

> In southern Lebanon there were a number of junctions,
> large villages and, closer to the border with Israel, key
> regions which we took on the first night when we spoke
> about a security belt. If we go from west to east the
> region of Ras al-Bayyadah, on the seashore; in the center
> we have the Maroun al-Ras-Bint Jabayl area; opposite
> Rahim and Misgav'Am we have At-Taiyba ridge and on the
> Fatahland front, what we call the Naqurim ridge--a ridge
> that controls the roads coming from 'Abaqah south.   On
> this front they split further south to the region of
> Metulla. These territories must be controlled by some
> force or another if we want to prevent terrorist activity
> on the northern front.[10]

By the end of the first day Israel had secured that which Major
Haddad's militia had failed to provide: a buffer zone, ranging in
depth from five to twenty kilometers, stretching from the
Mediterranean Sea to the foothills of Mount Hermon. It appeared
that the operation had ended.

Between 16 and 18 March, Israeli forces continued to make
small advances in those areas where the security belt was thinner
than ten kilometers.[11] Concerned about casualties, the IDF
abandoned its traditional practice of high mobility, choosing
instead to advance its mechanized infantry very cautiously behind
a devastating wall of artillery fire. Although that technique did
indeed minimize Israeli casualties,[12] it maximized non-combatant
deaths and civil destruction, and permitted the greak bulk of
enemy commandos to cross the Litani River to relative safety.
According to the military-affairs writer of the Jerusalem Post,
"The Israeli Army, once renowned for its Davidian finesse, was
used as a huge, stomping Goliath, hitting with all its might at
places from which the terrorists had already fled."[13]

On 19 March, with the operation seemingly ended, the IDF suddenly broke out of the newly created buffer zone toward the Litani River. According to one Israeli source, the new advance "was designed to carve out a PLO-free security belt in the 1,200 square kilometers between Israel's northern border and the Litani River."[14] Yet the IDF completely bypassed PLO concentrations around Tyre, thereby creating an enclave known as the "Tyre Pocket," which held out until June 1982. The expanded operation was explained in terms of tactical military necessity by General Gur, who emphasized the importance of controlling access to southern Lebanon across the Litani bridges ("Whoever holds these territories can control, in a satisfactory manner, what happens on the routes to southern Lebanon").[15] However, it was international politics that played the crucial role in the decision to expand the operation. On 19 March 1978, hours after the IDF began to move toward the Litani, the UN Security Council adopted Resolution 425. The two key points of the resolution, which was sponsored by the US, were (1) a call upon Israel to immediately "cease its military action against Lebanese territorial integrity and withdraw forthwith its forces from all Lebanese territory"; and (2) the establishment of a "United Nations interim force for southern Lebanon" (subsequently known as UNIFIL--United Nations Interim Force in Lebanon), for the purpose of "confirming the withdrawal of Israeli forces, restoring international peace and security and assisting the Government of Lebanon in ensuring the return of its effective authority in the area."[16] The Israeli thrust toward the Litani was therefore seen in many quarters "as a burst aimed at achieving as much as possible before the vote on the proposed UN Security Council Resolution."[17] Even General Gur acknowledged on 19 March that "We are not talking about a security belt any more, but about a general agreement in the area."[18] Phase II of the Israeli invasion was aimed at giving Israel the best possible bargaining position in the pursuit of a "general agreement."

The political objective of the expanded operation was quickly achieved. On 20 March, Israeli Defense Minister Ezer Weizman and General Gur met with General Siilasvuo, Commander of UNTSO, and Major General Erskine, newly-appointed UNIFIL commander. Despite Israel's vehement opposition to the US-sponsored Resolution 425, the four men quickly reached agreement on its implementation. It was reported that three points were established: (1) the area between the Litani and a line running from Ras al Biyada to Ibil as Saqy--roughly the area overrun by the IDF in the second stage of the invasion--would become a buffer zone; (2) UNIFIL would be responsible for patrolling the buffer zone; and (3) the strip of land lying between the Israeli-Lebanese boundary and the UNIFIL buffer zone would be designated a "peace zone" to be patrolled by the militia of Major Haddad and (eventually) units of the Lebanese Army. Israel would be permitted to continue its "good fence program" with the Lebanese inhabitants of the border region.[19] Consequently, instead of being pressured into turning over its ten-kilometer "security belt" to UNIFIL, Israel simply bargained away its additional conquests of 19 March, thereby buying time in which to solidify Major Haddad's grip on the strip of Lebanese territory immediately adjacent to the border. Israel declared a unilateral ceasefire on 21 March.[20]

Despite the widespread physical destruction visited upon southern Lebanon between 15 and 21 March by Israeli artillery and airstrikes--including the near-total destruction of Bint Jubayl and several other Shi'a villages[21] -- it was estimated that the anti-Israeli commandos lost only between 200 and 300 men out of a total force in southern Lebanon of approximately 10,000.[22] That figure represents relatively insignificant combatant losses in the context of an operation that caused the deaths of about 1,000 Arab [23] civilians and which, according to the Jerusalem Post, sent 100,000 civilians (about 40 percent of the southern Lebanese population in March 1978) fleeing to the north for their lives.[24] Given the practice of near-total reliance on artillery and airstrikes by the IDF--tactics described as "unprofessional" by the London Sunday Telegraph[25]--it can be reasonably concluded that operation "Stone of Wisdom" was designed not to inflict a conclusive military defeat on the fedayeen and leftist commandos, but to create new facts in southern Lebanon. These facts may be summarized as follows: (1) the securing in Lebanese territory of a security belt along the entire length of the boundary, not just in areas populated by Christians; (2) the occupation of the rest of southern Lebanon (except for the "Tyre Pocket") by an international force, on whose shoulders would fall the burden of preventing new commando infiltration; and (3) a new appreciation by the inhabitants of southern Lebanon--eighty percent of whose villages were damaged or destroyed by Israeli bombing and shelling[26]--of the dire consequences of trafficking with those who would attack Jewish towns and villages. Asked whether or not the Israeli invasion could be considered a success, an unnamed Western military expert replied, "If it was meant to drive the Palestinians out of the south and denude the area of its civilian population, the operation was a complete success. But if it was meant to destroy the guerrilla movement...then it was a complete failure."[27]

The first contingent of UNIFIL entered Lebanon by way of Israel on 22 March 1978,[28] and in the months of April through June the international force began to take up positions south of the Litani.[29] The Israeli withdrawal called for by Resolution 425 took place very slowly and in several stages beginning on 11 April. By 30 April Israel had turned over to UNIFIL some 550 square kilometers of Lebanese territory overrun between 10-21 March and was left in control of the security belt seized during the first phase of the invasion.[30]

With regard to the evacuation of the security belt itself, Israel dragged its feet. It insisted that UNIFIL take full responsibility for preventing the reintroduction of commandos south of the Litani and outside of the "Tyre Pocket."[31] Although UNIFIL was created primarily for the purpose of "confirming the withdrawal of Israeli forces," Israel's position coincided with that of the Lebanese Government, which was once again showing great reluctance to send army units to the troubled south. According to an unnamed Lebanese senior official, "We see Resolution 425 referring to the return of Lebanon's effective authority in the area as meaning the removal of any armed forces that are present without our authorization," Palestinians as well as Israelis.[32] Despite the cooperation of Palestine Liberation Organization Chairman Yasir Arafat, fedayeen elements apparently not under his control sniped at UNIFIL positions and launched rockets at Israeli settlements from positions north of the Litani River.[33] UNIFIL's position became increasingly difficult, as members of the peacekeeping force found themselves being harassed not only by Palestinians, but by Major Haddad's militia as well.[34]

Israel took the position that although it had no claim on Lebanese territory, it would leave Lebanon only "when it was certain that UNIFIL was strong enough to prevent attacks on Israel from Lebanon."[35] Under strong international pressure, Israel, on 21 May, finally set a firm date for its withdrawal from Lebanon: 13 June 1978. The withdrawal, according to Israeli Cabinet Secretary Ayre Naor, would be unconditional, but Israel would be obliged to "take measures to ensure the security of the local Christian Lebanese population."[36]

On 13 June, as promised, the IDF ended its ninety-one-day occupation of southern Lebanon. In a military ceremony at Mays al Jabal the Israeli flag was lowered.[37] However, the security belt occupied by Israel since 15 March was handed over not to UNIFIL, but to Major Saad Haddad and his militia. As Israel's northern commander Major General Avigdor Ben-Gal explained, "The Israeli Government is insisting upon its commitment to protect the Christian minority in southern Lebanon."[38] Accordingly, Major Haddad's militia was given responsibility for securing the entire border, from Al Khiyam to Ra's al Biyada.[39] The militia would henceforth secure for Israel a strip of Lebanese territory ranging in depth from five to eight kilometers, with an even larger bulge in the Marj 'Uyun area.

As one observer noted, the transfer of the security belt to Haddad by Israel raised the "central question" of "the chain of command between the Lebanese Government and Haddad."[40] If Haddad were not Beirut's official representative in the south, Israel's action would clearly have been contrary to the will of the Security Council as expressed by Resolution 425. Yet President Sarkis, hoping to mollify the extreme Maronite nationalists in Lebanon, accorded provisional recognition to Haddad,[41] thereby granting a measure of legitimacy to Israel's action.

The question of Major Haddad's attitude toward the Government of Lebanon however, remained, unanswered for the time being. Although President Sarkis was willing to accord an aura of legitimacy to Haddad, he also wanted to dispatch Lebanese regulars to the border areas in order to supplement the rightist militia. With characteristic caution Sarkis dispatched several Lebanese officers to meet with their Israeli counterparts at the UNIFIL Headquarters at An Naqurah to discuss the impending southern movement of the Lebanese Army.[42] During the meeting, which took place on 30 July 1978, Israel issued four guidelines for the southern deployment of Lebanese regulars: (1) the position of Major Haddad must be officially recognized by the Lebanese Government; (2) units of the Lebanese Army could be deployed only outside the Christian border enclaves; (3) no Syrian officers or advisors could accompany the Lebanese; and (4) no interference with the "good fence program" would be tolerated.[43]

The nature of the demands made it clear that Israel would accept no Lebanese military deployment along the border except under conditions that would make the Sarkis regime--still propped by Syria--an active accomplice in the Israeli security plan for the border region. Points (1) and (3) probably could have been accepted by Sarkis inasmuch as he had already provisionally recognized Haddad, and the Syrians had no particular desire to challenge the Israeli "red line" policy. Yet points (2) and (4) were clearly aimed at luring Sarkis into an arrangement whereby the Christian enclaves would be Lebanese in name only. Had he accepted the Israeli conditions Sarkis would have undermined the already tenuous domestic position of Syria's Assad and enraged the Lebanese National Movement. Israel was in the ideal position of having nothing to lose regardless of Sarkis' choice.

On 31 July 1978 the Lebanese President dispatched a 650-man army battalion from Ablah, in the central Biqa', to the south. The unit planned to establish its headquarters in Tibnin, a village north of Bint Jubayl and outside the Israeli security belt. The Lebanese soldiers reportedly received enthusiastic receptions in the villages of the Biqa' as they marched south. The cheering stopped at Kawkaba, however, as the battalion came under an artillery attack by Major Haddad's militia. By entering Kawkaba the Lebanese unit indicated its intention of moving to Tibnin by way of the Christian enclave in the vicinity of Marj 'Uyun, a violation of point (2) of the Israeli guidelines. In fact Israeli television blamed Sarkis for provoking the shelling by having the unit attempt to pass through Christian territory rather than through Nabatiyah. Apparently, the guidelines were meant to be taken quite literally. Rather than redirecting the unit so as to conform to the march plan established for it by Israel, the Lebanese Defense Ministry ordered the expeditionary force back to its barracks.[44]

If the abortive movement of Lebanon's Army to the south accomplished nothing else, it clearly demonstrated the intentions of Major Haddad. The pretense of loyalty to the Lebanese Government--an illusion that had been maintained by Haddad, Sarkis, and Begin--was finished. The military-affairs writer of the Jerusalem Post, Hirsh Goodman, blamed both Haddad and the Israeli Government for the continuing mess in southern Lebanon. According to Goodman, Haddad's extremely close relationship with Israeli military commanders was subverting the Begin government's policy toward southern Lebanon. Goodman noted Israel's willingness to permit the Lebanese Army to patrol roads on the periphery of the Christian enclaves, but he observed that Haddad would not even go along with that. The IDF, complained Goodman, seemed to be willing to grant Haddad's every wish. Goodman concluded his analysis with the following observation:

> Major Haddad should be made to realize that moderation is a price he has to pay--in the interest of ultimate stability in southern Lebanon, and in order to ensure the continuation of the Israeli support upon which he has been able to rely until now.[45]

The distinct possibility existed, however, that southern Lebanon had become for Israel a stage upon which a scene far more important than those played over the past six decades in the Upper Galilee was being acted out. Perhaps Mr. Goodman missed the point in assuming that Israel sought "stability" in southern Lebanon and that a renegade Lebanese Army Major was clumsily undermining the moderate policies of Mr. Begin. As James M. Markham has noted,

> As long as southern Lebanon remains unstable, the rest of Lebanon remains unstable; in the south artillery shells have been exploding daily, killing people, but farther north, in the beautiful mountains above Beirut, one can hear Bashir Gemayal's the Phalangist military chief militiamen practicing with mortars and automatic weapons. Guns continue to be shipped into the Maronite port of Juniye, and there had been occasional sharp clashes...between Syrian peacekeepers and Christian militia. "Many of us do not consider that this war has ended," says Charles Malik a leading Lebanese Christian ideologue calmly.[46]

NOTES

1. Arab Report and Record, 1-15 March 1978, No. 5, pp. 185-186.

2. Ibid., p. 162.

3. Ibid.

4. Hirsh Goodman, "Israel Forces Holding Southern Lebanon," Jerusalem Post (International Edition), 21 March 1978, p. 7.

5. Arab Report and Record, 1-15 March 1978, No. 5, p. 184.

6. Goodman, "Israel Forces Holding Southern Lebanon," p.7.

7. Ibid.

8. Ibid.

9. Arab Report and Record, 16-31 March 1978, No. 6, p. 200.

10. "Press Conference with Ezer Weizman & Mordechai Gur," Jerusalem Domestic Service, 20 March 1978 (Foreign Broadcast Information Service, 21 March 1978, pp. N3-N5)

11. Arab Report and Record, 16-31 March 1978, No. 6, pp. 222-223.

12. The IDF suffered only eighteen deaths during the operation. Newsweek, 3 April 1978, p. 39.

13. As quoted in Newsweek, 3 April 1978, p. 42.

14. Anan Safadi, Jerusalem Post Magazine, 7 April 1978, p. 4.

15. "Press Conference with Ezer Weizman and Mordechai Gur, p. N4.

16. The complete text of Resolution 425 may be found in Arab Report and Record, 16-31 March 1978, No. 6, p. 221.

17. Ibid., p. 224.

18. Ibid.

19. Ibid., p. 225.

20. Ibid.

21. "They the Israelis also seemed to be engaging in a general leveling of almost every significant structure in the occupied area..." Newsweek, 27 March 1978, p. 40.

22. John K. Cooley, "PLO-Israeli Strife Shakes Uneasy Peace in Lebanon," Christian Science Monitor, 7 April 1978, p. 4.

23. According to a survey by the International Committee of the Red Cross, as reported in the Arab Report and Record, 16-31 March 1978, No. 6, p. 222.

24. Jerusalem Post (International Edition), 21 March 1978, p. 2.

25. As quoted in the Arab Report and Record, 16-31 March 1978, No.6, p. 222.

26. According to a survey by the International Committee of the Red Cross, as reported in the Arab Report and Record, 1-15 April 1978 No. 7, p. 247.

27. As quoted in Newsweek, 3 April 1978, p. 42.

28. Arab Report and Record, 16-31 March 1978, No. 6, p. 225.

29. John K. Cooley, "UN Faces an Uncertain Role in South Lebanon," Christian Science Monitor, 22 March 1978, p. 34.

30. Arab Report and Record, 16-30 April 1978, No. 8, p. 313.

31. Cooley, "UN Faces an Uncertain Role in South Lebanon," p. 34.

32. Marvine Howe, "PLO Reports Raids on Israeli Troops," New York Times, 26 March 1978, p. 10.

33. Cooley, "PLO-Israeli Strife Shakes Uneasy Peace in Lebanon," p. 4.

34. Arab Report and Record, 1-15 April 1978, No. 7, p. 248.

35. Facts on File, 21 April 1978, p. 274.

36. Arab Report and Record, 16-31 May 1978, No. 10, p. 389.

37. "Israel Leaves Southern Lebanon," Christian Science Monitor, 14 June 1978, p. 3.

38. Ibid.

39. Arab Report and Record, 1-15 June 1978, No. 11, p. 427.

40. Louis Wiznitzer, "UN Troops Sitting on a 'Volcano' Now That the Israelis Have Pulled Out," Christian Science Monitor, 15 June 1978, p. 6.

41. Ibid.

42. Hirsh Goodman, "Israel 'Guidelines' for Lebanese Troops," Jerusalem Post (International Edition), 1 August 1978, pp. 1-2.

43. Ibid.

44. Arab Report and Record, 16-31 July 1978, No. 14, p. 518, and Francis Ofner, "Lebanon Christians Block Army Drive," Christian Science Monitor, 1 August 1978, pp. 1, 10. According to Ofner, the Syrian Minister of Information had stated on 29 July 1978 that the Lebanese unit would have arrested Haddad and his deputy, Shidiaq, and closed the "good fence."

45. Hirsh Goodman, "Muddling Along in Lebanon," Jerusalem Post (International Edition), 15 August 1978, p. 8.

46. James M. Markham, "The War That Won't Go Away," New York Times Magazine, 9 October 1977, p. 52.

10. The South Lebanon Pressure Point

It is difficult to overstate the magnitude of Prime Minister Begin's achievement with regard to southern Lebanon in the spring of 1978. He succeeded in doing that which none of his predecessors in Jerusalem--Israeli or British--ever came close to achieving: the establishment on Lebanese soil of a security shield for northern Israel. The shield was double-layered: a fully connected border strip run by Major Haddad (who declared the "independence" of "Free Lebanon" on 18 April 1979); and to the north of Haddad's enclave, UNIFIL, which eventually reached a total strength of approximately 6,000. True, Israel was still within the range of PLO gunners in the Tyre Pocket and Beaufort Castle areas. Yet the feasibility of successful ground infiltration--a politically explosive issue in Israel despite its traditionally low success rate--was reduced even further.

Notwithstanding Begin's success, the years leading up to the cataclysmic invasion of June 1982 were by no means peaceful for the south of Lebanon. Why, given the success of the March 1978 operation, did southern Lebanon remain the scene of widespread violence for several more years?

Hirsh Goodman's analysis of Israeli support for Major Haddad, presented in the previous chapter, probably provides the key for understanding why chaos persisted. Were it simply a matter of border security, Israel would have lost nothing by instructing Major Haddad to subordinate his forces to the Lebanese Armed Forces. Yet by supporting (or, more plausibly, directing) Haddad's defiance of the Government of Lebanon, Israel was obviously thinking about issues which transcended border security. Southern Lebanon had become, in the words of James Markham, "a highly useful pressure point for Israeli diplomacy, and instability in the south keeps both Assad and the Palestinians off balance."[1] Beyond putting the Syrians and the PLO on the defensive, Israeli support of Haddad also indicated a growing interest on the part of the Begin government in influencing the future shape of the Lebanese body politic itself. Specifically, the Israel-Haddad connection was an integral part of Israel's growing relationship with the predominantly Maronite Lebanese Front, a coalition of organizations representing one set of contestants in the Lebanese civil war. The Lebanese Front and its militia--the Lebanese Forces--came to be dominated by Bashir Gemayel, the son of the founder of the Lebanese Phalange Party, Pierre Gemayel.

This is not to say that Israel was obsessed with the idea of creating a Maronite mini-state or installing an Israeli puppet as the President of the Republic. As one prominent Maronite politician and militia leader commented to the author, "The Israelis gave us sufficient arms and training to help us to our knees, but they never gave us enough so that we could stand on our

feet."[2] In a 1982 interview Yitzhak Rabin, former Prime Minister
of Israel, defined his government's aid to the Christian militias
in terms of "only supplies of arms and training of the fighting
Christians in the use of them....I made it clear that the basic
principle would be to help them to help themselves."[3] Aid to the
Lebanese Forces, combined with encouragement of Major Haddad's
obstreperous behavior, helped to keep the Lebanese pot boiling by
exacerbating intra-Lebanese tensions at the expense of a paralyzed
central government. Thus, the ambition of Bashir Gemayel and his
colleagues to create and rule a "New Lebanon" was harnessed in
support of an Israeli policy designed to harass the PLO and keep
Syria preoccupied with a no-win stability operation in Lebanon.

The ultimate decision of the Israelis to clear the way for
Bashir Gemayel's election to the Lebanese presidency appears to
have been the by-product of another decision deemed by Israeli
policymakers to be far more significant: the decision to
annihilate the PLO as an independent political force, an
independence derived from the territorial status of the PLO in
Lebanon.   In certain parts of the country--from southwest Beirut
down to Tyre, from the mouth of the Qasimiyyah across to Nabatiyah
and up into the Arqub--the PLO's writ was law. Yasir Arafat was
free to travel the world harvesting endorsements and opening
"embassies" and then return to Beirut, a base from which he could
operate with relative independence. As the 1980s approached, two
trends emerged to hasten the final reckoning: a growing tendency
of many states to recognize the PLO's status as the legitimate
representative of Palestinian nationalism, a status derived in
part from Arafat's image as a totally dedicated, independent
spokesman for the rights of his people; and the determination of
the Begin government, in the wake of the Camp David Accords and
subsequent evacuation of the Sinai Peninsula, to hold onto the
West Bank by encouraging Jewish colonization and Palestinian
emigration.

From the Israeli perspective the PLO, lurking in its Lebanese
sanctuary, was an obstacle to the government's West Bank policy.
An independent PLO could "blackmail" the Arab residents of the
West Bank into rejecting Israeli autonomy plans and opposing the
Israeli-inspired Village Leagues, composed as they were of
Palestinians opposed to the PLO. By destroying Arafat's military
apparatus, thereby dislodging him from his "state within a state"
in Beirut and southern Lebanon, the PLO's claim to be the
independent, legitimate representative of all Palestinians could
not possibly remain valid. The scattered remnants of the PLO
would be snatched up by competing Arab states, and the Arabs of
the Occupied Territories would finally realize the inevitability
of permanent Israeli rule. Regardless of how the PLO is viewed--
terrorists or freedom fighters, blackmailers or nationalists--
stripped of its territorial base it would no longer be capable of
inspiring opposition to Begin's policy of creeping annexation.

Although Arafat's military apparatus made possible his roles
as Arab leader, international statesman, guerrilla fighter, and

Third-World luminary, it suffered from two fatal weaknesses. Its
first weakness was its absolute inability to successfully defend
any position Israeli forces were determined to take. This is not
to denigrate the skill or dedication of the individual Palestinian
fighter. But since the mid-1970s Israel had been able to handily
defeat any combination of Arab countries arrayed against it.
Thus, the prospects for success of the approximately 15,000
fighters at Arafat's disposal until 1982 must be recognized as
slim indeed. Its second weakness was the proclivity of Arafat
and his military to be drawn into the whirlpool of Lebanese
politics. Alliances had been formed between the PLO and the
organizations making up the Lebanese National Movement, the
predominantly Muslim counterweight to the overwhelmingly Christian
Lebanese Front. One such alliance had grave consequences for the
PLO's prospects in southern Lebanon. The Organization for
Communist Action in Lebanon (OCAL), led by a Shi'a (Muhsin
Ibrahim) and composed mostly of Shi'a, was locked in a deadly
battle for preeminence within the Shi'a community against Amal,
the organization founded by the presumably murdered Imam Musa
Sadr. In southern Lebanon Amal chapters held sway in the
overwhelming majority of Shi'a villages. Yet the PLO was allied
with OCAL. By early 1982 Amal was shooting it out regularly with
OCAL and the PLO in the south. Indeed, the gradual alienation of
the south Lebanon Shi'a population from the PLO was one of the
major themes of the late 1970s and early 1980s. The destruction
wrought by the Israeli operation of March 1978 undoubtedly
convinced many residents of the south that the PLO's presence in
populated areas was an unfailing harbinger of death and
destruction at the hands of Israel or Haddad. This impression was
not ameliorated by the tendency of PLO fighters--a tendency
inherently present in armies of occupation--to act with arrogance
and high-handedness toward the inhabitants of the region.
Furthermore, once the Israelis had consolidated his expanded
enclave for him in 1978, Haddad was able, with Israeli assistance,
to recruit Shi'a in significant numbers into his militia.
Although his militiamen may not always have been drawn from the
cream of Shi'a youth, they nevertheless came to compose some sixty
percent of Haddad's "regulars."[4] In sum, the residents of southern
Lebanon were quite prepared by 1982 to see the PLO swept out once
and for all.

UNIFIL, whose headquarters at An Naqura was within Haddad's
"Free Lebanon," had the unenviable task of interposing itself
between Haddad and the PLO. It was provoked and suffered
casualties at the hands of both sides. Its weaker were often
singled out for special harassment. Although the Israeli
government developed a grudging respect for some of the UNIFIL
units and acknowledged that UNIFIL was often effective in
frustrating Palestinian infiltration of Haddad's enclave,[5]
UNIFIL's fundamental problem was that its charter was directly
contrary to the Israeli "pressure point" strategy in southern
Lebanon. In a sensible move which nevertheless symbolized its

impotence in the face of Israeli determination, UNIFIL gingerly stepped aside when Israeli forces swept past on their way to Beirut in June 1982.

The penultimate step toward the clearing of the PLO from southern Lebanon occurred in July 1981. From 10-24 July, Israel conducted an intensive aerial campaign against PLO positions between Sidon and Nabatiyah, also knocking out highway bridges throughout the south. On 15 July the PLO retaliated with artillery and rocket barrages against northern Israel, bombardments which, according to the IDF spokesman, "forced 60,000 Galileans to stay underground in shelters."[6] The Israeli campaign and PLO response ended on 24 July with a ceasefire arranged by Ambassador Philip Habib, President Reagan's special negotiator for the Middle East.

Many observers deemed the Habib ceasefire to be a political gain for the PLO. Although Arafat did not deal directly with the US or Israel, the PLO was undeniably a party to the arrangement. Having handed Arafat a political victory in return for the cessation of hostilities which it initiated, and having suffered a public relations beating as a result of the bombing of a Beirut residential area on 17 July, the Begin government embarked on a course designed to neutralize the PLO once and for all.

During the ceasefire southern Lebanon remained in a state of turmoil. Haddad harassed UNIFIL and periodically shelled populated areas from his enclave, whose own residents also suffered from artillery attacks. The PLO found itself increasingly embroiled in fights with Amal in support of its OCAL allies. In order not to give the Israelis a pretext to attack, the PLO refrained from launching ground and artillery attacks against Israeli territory. Had border security been the Israeli goal, the Habib ceasefire would have constituted another victory for the Begin government.

Yet the issue had moved beyond border security, as Israel prepared to crush the PLO's military forces in southern Lebanon. It was, of course, in Israel's interests to portray offensive military operations as a defensive reaction to threats against the security of Israel and Jews worldwide. The following statement by David Kimche, Director-General of the Israeli Foreign Ministry, illustrates the public Israeli stand quite adequately:

> After Mr. Habib brought about an agreement for the cessation of hostilities in July 1981, the PLO set about strengthening their military infrastructure in southern Lebanon, thus making the Peace for Galilee Operation inevitable. At a time when we respected the Habib agreement, the PLO built fortifications, brought up heavy guns and arms, and repeatedly infiltrated Israel in order to lay mines, place bombs in civilian centers, attack transport, etc. At the same time, Jews abroad increasingly became a target for attack--a synagogue in

Vienna, a busload of Jewish children in Antwerp, an Ambassador in London. All this by an organization dedicated to our destruction, which no one was willing to curb or rebuke. This, then, forms the back-drop to our operation against the PLO in Lebanon, which was designed to defend the lives of our citizens and to remove the threat which the military infrastructure of the PLO had become.[7]

There are, of course, several aspects of Mr. Kimche's statement which require some elaboration. First, the resupply of PLO forces in southern Lebanon--a rather ordinary course of action for a military commander given a respite from hostilities initiated by the enemy--seems to have had no effect on the Israeli blitzkreig of June 1982. This, arguably, is a case of 20-20 hindsight. Yet the author knows of no serious military analyst who argued prior to 6 June 1982 that the PLO military forces constituted an offensive conventional threat against Israel. Second, there is no record of any PLO infiltration of Israel by way of Lebanese territory during the life of the Habib ceasefire. Third, there is no evidence that the PLO was responsible for the attacks on Jews listed by Mr. Kimche, or that such attacks were germane to the ceasefire arranged by Ambassador Habib. The shooting of the Israeli Ambassador in London, Mr. Argov (which served as the proximate cause for the invasion of Lebanon on 6 June 1982) was carried out by Arab assailants who, according to the British Prime Minister, Mrs. Thatcher, also intended to shoot the PLO's London representative.[8] It appears that the organization responsible for the act is based in Syria, violently opposes Yasir Arafat, and, according to a columnist normally disposed quite favorably toward Israel, has received some funding from one of the Israeli intelligence services for the purpose of wreaking havoc within Palestinian political circles.[9]

On 3 June 1982 Ambassador Argov was shot and critically injured. On 4 June, Israeli air attacks began against Palestinian camps in the Beirut area. On the same day, PLO gunners opened up on northern Israel, killing one Israeli and wounding four. On 6 June the invasion was on.

Unlike the March 1978 operation, the June 1982 invasion featured speed. Enjoying overwhelming superiority in every respect, Israeli forces reached the outskirts of Beirut by 8 June. After routing Syrian units located southeast of Jazzin, Israeli units attained full control of the southern Biqa' by 11 June. Unlike the Australian operation of 1941, the Israelis in June 1982 also sent a column straight up past Jazzin, through the mountains of the Shuf, reaching Ayn Dara (just south of the Beirut-Damascus Highway) by 8 June. Within less than six days of fighting, the IDF had taken control of about 4,500 square kilometers of Lebanese territory and had all but liquidated the PLO military presence in southern Lebanon.

The stated Israeli objective of Operation Peace for Galilee was to remove all PLO military assets from artillery range (twenty-five miles) of Israel. This rationale constituted a reformulation of the traditional border-security argument, a concern which does not appear to have actually motivated Israeli policymakers. This actual objective became evident when the IDF subsequently laid siege to west Beirut and subjected parts of the city to heavy air and artillery bombardments. Arafat, commanding several thousand PLO fighters trapped in the city, eventually agreed to evacuate his forces in accordance with yet another agreement brokered by Mr. Habib. Between 21 August and 6 September 1982, the PLO evacuated Beirut, effectively shutting down the "state within a state" which had been growing on Lebanese soil for over a decade.

Bashir Gemayel, who had disappointed his Israeli allies by not throwing his Lebanese forces into the battle against the PLO, became Lebanon's President-elect on 23 August, but was assassinated on 14 September 1982 before assuming office. On the following day Israeli forces entered Beirut, and on 16 through 18 September Lebanese militiamen massacred several hundred unarmed Palestinian and Lebanese inhabitants of the Sabra and Shatila refugee camps on the outskirts of the capital.

NOTES

1. James M. Markham, "The War That Won't Go Away," New York Times Magazine, 9 October 1977, p. 52.

2. Statement made to the author, March 1983.

3. As quoted by Naomi Joy Weinberger in "Peacekeeping Options in Lebanon," The Middle East Journal, Vol. 37 No.3 Summer 1983, p. 347.

4. Ibid., p. 346.

5. "For all of Haddad's accusations that UNIFIL did not deter the PLO, it is worthy of note that Major Haddad never caught a single PLO infiltrator whereas UNIFIL stopped scores of guerrillas over the years." Ibid.

6. IDF Spokesman, Operation Peace For Galilee (undated briefing paper), p. 6.

7. David Kimche, "Lebanon: The Hour of Truth," Middle East Insight, Volume Three, No. 1, 1983, p.6.

8. New York Times, 7 June 1982, p. 13.

9. Jack Anderson, "Terrorist Wages One-Man War Against Israel," <u>Washington Post</u>, 25 April 1983.

11. The May 1983 Israeli-Lebanese Agreement

On 28 December 1982 talks aimed at securing the evacuation of Israeli forces from Lebanon talks opened in Khaldah, Lebanon between Israeli, Lebanese, and American representatives. Several months of arduous negotiations produced an agreement[1] which was signed on 17 May 1983, and later abrogated by the Lebanese parliament on 5 March 1984. The agreement was not immediately implemented because of the continued presence of Syrian and PLO forces in Lebanon; neither Syria nor the PLO were parties to the agreement. Ghassan Tueni, former Lebanese Ambassador to the UN, stated that "By rendering its withdrawal from Lebanon contingent upon Syrian and Palestinian withdrawals," Israel "bestowed Syria and the PLO with a veto power, almost a veto right over the Lebanese-Israeli Agreement."[2]

This analysis will focus on the merits of the 1983 agreement in the historical context of the Lebanon-Palestine/Israel frontier. It proceeds on the assumption that its provisions may form the basis for future discussions on bilateral security arrangements.

Leaving aside the question of the withdrawal of other parties from Lebanon, the agreement itself rested upon one fundamental proposition: in return for a promised complete withdrawal of Israeli forces from Lebanon, the Government of Lebanon would implement specified "security arrangements" designed to detect and prevent "hostile activities" and the introduction or movement toward the Israeli border of "unauthorized armed men or military equipment". Presumably Israel would have refused to withdraw from Lebanese territory had the Lebanese Government, such as it is, declined to make certain commitments with regard to the security of northern Israel. The invasion was, after all, called Operation Peace for Galilee.

If, by the late 1970s, Israel's approach to southern Lebanon had become characterized by geopolitical "pressure point" tactics rather than traditional concerns about infiltration, and if the 1982 invasion had more to do with creating new geopolitical facts than with providing "Peace for Galilee," is it correct to assume that, having smashed the PLO, Israel has now reverted to the pre-Begin attitude toward southern Lebanon? With the PLO gone, is Israel's major concern that of providing border security?

If the question is rephrased along the lines of "Would Israel, under the terms of the May 1983 agreement with Lebanon, have retained the ability to destabilize Lebanon by manipulating events in the south," the answer is yes. Whether Israel has any such intention now, or is likely to develop such intentions in the future, is moot. It can, of course, be argued that Israel can do anything it likes to Lebanon with or without an agreement, that American interests in the Middle East dictate that Israel be eased

FIGURE 11.1: SECURITY ZONES:
MAY 17 AGREEMENT

out of Lebanon under the least onerous terms attainable, and that the agreement, stopping as it did short of a Peace Treaty, would have done exactly that. It can also be argued that the US is in no position to require an Israeli withdrawal in the absence of security arrangements acceptable to the Israeli government. These are, of course, issues and questions which transcend the scope of this study.

The agreement terminated the "state of war" between the two parties and affirmed the inviolability of the "existing international boundary between Lebanon and Israel." Thus, the 1949 GAA was abrogated, and Israel for the first time formally accepted the 1923 boundary accord. It would also appear that Israel renounced its self-proclaimed right to conduct military operations on Lebanese territory.

Both sides committed themselves to preventing their territory from being "used as a base for hostile or terrorist activity against the other party, its territory or its people," by preventing "the existence or organization of irregular forces, armed bands, organizations, bases, offices or infrastructures, the aims and purposes of which include incursions or any act of terrorism into the territory of the other party, or any other activity aimed at threatening or endangering the security of the other party and safety of its people." This particular provision went on to say that "all agreements and arrangements enabling the presence and functioning on the territory of either party of elements hostile to the other party are null and void"; and as such it represented a significant expansion of parallel language contained in the 1949 GAA. The obvious result was the termination of the 1969 Cairo agreement between the Lebanese Government and the PLO. Would Jews living outside Israel, regardless of nationality, have been considered by Israel to be among the "people" to be protected by this provision? If so, the Government of Lebanon, whether it agreed to such an interpretation or not, could have found itself accused of a violation because of an incident taking place thousands of miles away, one allegedly involving a resident of Lebanon or the use of a Lebanese apartment building for "planning."

The agreement established a "security region" encompassing all Lebanese territory south of a line drawn north of Sidon (following the Awwali River) across Jabal Baruk, and across the Biqa' to a point on the Syrian border northeast of Rashayya. The security region was itself divided into two zones, A and B. Figure 11.1 depicts the security region.

Zone B comprised the southern part of the security region, from the border with Israel to the mouth of the Zahrani River and then below an easterly line drawn north of Nabatiyah and Marj 'Uyun, terminating where the Israeli ceasefire line on the Golan Heights meets the Lebanon boundary. Zone B would have been secured by a Lebanese territorial brigade with a personnel strength of 4,341. The territorial brigade would have

encompassed" the existing local units i.e., Haddad's forces
which had been formed into a near-brigade-sized unit, along with
Lebanese Army personnel from among the inhabitants of the security
region, in conformity with Lebanese Army regulations." The
agreement went on to say that all armed representatives of the
Lebanese Government in Zone B would be subordinated to the brigade
commander. Furthermore, no limitation was placed on the number of
armed, non-military official Lebanese elements operating in Zone
B.

Zone B--an area slightly larger than the Lebanese sector of
the 1949 Limited Forces Zone of the GAA--would have been permitted
considerably more security personnel than the 1,500 allowed by the
GAA. Yet it would appear that these security forces were to be
composed in large part of personnel who had been under Israeli
command for several years. The phrase "in conformity with
Lebanese Army regulations" might have provided the Lebanese
government with an escape clause relating to the integration of
some unsavory militia personnel into the army, as well as to the
limitation on integrating only inhabitants of the security region.
Whether or not the Lebanese would have resorted to legalisms is
not known, to say nothing of the possible Israeli reaction. Two
points with regard to Israeli intentions seem clear: first, the
executors of Israel's "pressure point" strategy of the past
several years would have been adorned with the cloak of Lebanese
legitimacy; and second, the security region--especially Zone B--
would have been different from the rest of Lebanon in the sense
that soldiers from Tripoli, or Baalbek, or Beirut could not have
served long-term assignments in places like Tyre, or Nabatiyah, or
Marj 'Uyun. What implications might this have had for a central
government whose "nation-building" efforts--pathetic as they
admittedly were --depended to a great extent on the deployment of
a national army? There may have been escape clauses allowing
Lebanon to introduce other army units into the security region for
training and also for "operational emergency situations" (but only
in accordance with procedures to be established by an Israeli-
Lebanese Security Arrangements Committee). Yet it is also
possible that the localism engendered presumably to assuage
Israeli security concerns would have further retarded the
development of a Lebanese nation-state and ensured the continued
existence of a useful pressure point, just in case the rest of
Lebanon went in a direction not to Israel's liking.

With one small exception "the only organized armed forces and
elements permitted in the security region" were those "organized
under the full authority of the Government of Lebanon." Excepted
was one unit of UNIFIL which, if Lebanon had so requested, could
have been stationed in the Sidon area to help "in asserting
governmental authority and protection in the Palestinian refugee
camp areas." Clearly this clause eliminated the possibility of
Israeli units being stationed on Lebanese territory. It also
meant, however, that Lebanon could not seek the assistance of
multinational forces in the security region, and it could not seek
a U.N. presence there beyond that authorized. As is the case

with other provisions of the agreement which tend to limit the
authority of the Lebanese government, it is difficult to measure
what the consequences may have been. With the U.N. and
multinational forces effectively banned from the security region,
future disputes in connection with the Israel-Lebanon frontier
would have to be adjudicated on a bilateral basis only, with the
US standing ready "to promote the expeditious resolution of
disputes arising out of the interpretation or application of the
present agreement."

Zone A was likewise permitted a Lebanese brigade for security
purposes, this one a "regular" unit of equal size to the
territorial brigade in Zone B. Both units were to have been
permitted all of the weapons and equipment organic to a Lebanese
Army brigade, including tanks, armored cars, armored personnel
carriers, artillery, mortars, antitank weapons, antiaircraft guns
(40-mm or less, not radar-guided), communications gear, and
surveillance equipment. With regard to the last item, the
Lebanese would have needed prior approval before employing ground
radars within ten kilometers of the border, and Lebanese ground
radars could not search across the boundary into Israel.

The only references to civilian cross-border movements and
other issues germane to the 1926 Good Neighbourly Relations Accord
were contained in Article 8. An Israeli-Lebanese Joint Liaison
Committee (with American participation) was to have been formed
which would "address itself on a continuing basis to the
development of mutual relations between Lebanon and Israel, inter
alia the regulation of the movement of goods, products and
persons, communications, etc." Six months after the withdrawal of
Israeli forces the parties were to have initiated negotiations
within the Joint Liaison Committee "in order to conclude
agreements on the movements of goods, products and persons" and to
ensure the implementation of the agreements.

The Joint Liaison Committee, whose decisions required
unanimity, would have dealt with unresolved security matters
reported to it by the Security Arrangements Committee (SAC),
composed of an equal number of Israeli and Lebanese
representatives and headed by senior officers. The SAC, which was
intended to meet on a biweekly basis alternately in Lebanon and
Israel, had three missions: to supervise the implementation of
all security arrangements, to establish and operate Joint
Supervisory Teams, and to try to resolve all problems arising from
the implementation of the security arrangements. The SAC would
have been the successor to the 1949 Israel-Lebanon Mixed Armistice
Commission (ILMAC), and its meetings were to be held in the
vicinity of the Lebanese towns of Hasbayya and Mayfadun, at
"Security Arrangements Supervision Centers" commanded by Lebanese
officers.

The eyes and ears of the SAC would have been the Joint
Supervisory Teams (JSTs), eight in number (maximum), and each
commanded by a Lebanese officer. The JSTs were supposed to be

Lebanese and Israeli in composition and were charged with
conducting "regular verification of the implementation of the
provisions of the security arrangements." They were not intended
to usurp the prerogatives of Lebanese law-enforcement personnel,
and they were "subject to termination upon ninety days notice by
either party given at any time after two years from the date of
entry into force of the present agreement." The JSTs were not to
use force except in self-defense, but they were authorized freedom
of movement throughout the security region and were to report
violations (actual or potential) to Lebanese authorities through
the Security Arrangements Supervision Centers. Operational
details of the JSTs were to have been worked out by the SAC. As a
further safety measure the annex to the agreement mandated "direct
radio and telephone communications between the respective military
commanders and their staffs in the immediate border region, as
well as face-to-face consultations."

In sum, the agreement of 17 May 1983 went far beyond the 1949
GAA in both specificity and breadth. Unlike the armistice it had
an element of one-sidedness in that the security arrangements all
pertained to Lebanese territory. It deferred questions related
to the cross-border movement of civilian goods, products, and
persons, but sought to institutionalize regular contacts between
Lebanese and Israeli military personnel at several levels. It
would appear that had the Lebanese Government been able and
willing to govern the south, and if the Israeli government had
chosen to focus exclusively on the bland basics of border
security, this agreement could have overcome the nightmarish
security problems so evident from 1936-39 and again in the 70s and
80s. If the two parties had failed to perform in this manner, the
agreement could not have guaranteed that the south of Lebanon
would have remained peaceful. Rather its provisions, particularly
those which tended to emphasize the differences between the
security region and the rest of Lebanon, could conceivably have
been used by any party seeking to foment instability in Lebanon to
do so with a veneer of legality and legitimacy. In order to
minimize the effects of just such an eventuality, the United
States--whose role as a mediator was written into the agreement--
would have been obliged to maintain a lively interest in the
Israeli-Lebanese frontier.

As a result of talks held in Damascus in early March 1984
between Presidents Asad of Syria and Gemayel of Lebanon, the
Lebanese cabinet decided on 5 March 1984 to abrogate the agreement
of 17 May 1983. According to a Beirut Domestic Service Broadcast
of 5 March 1984, the cabinet issued the following statement:

> The Lebanese Government will take the necessary steps
> that will lead to the government's laying down security
> measures and arrangements that would ensure sovereignty,
> security, and stability in southern Lebanon; that would
> prevent infiltration through the southern borders; and
> that would achieve the withdrawal of the Israeli forces
> from all Lebanese territory.[3]

On 9 March 1984 Israeli Prime Minister Shamir made the following response to a question concerning the agreement's abrogation:

> The abrogation of the accord relieves us of the commitments we had undertaken as part of the agreement. In the long months of negotiations... we gave up some demands tevi'ot pertaining primarily to the security arrangements. From now on these limitations will no longer apply to us.[4]

Notwithstanding Shamir's defiant tone, the abrogation of the agreement left Israel in a difficult position. Having invaded Lebanon under the pretext of securing "peace for Galilee," it could not very easily just pack up and leave without establishing some mechanism for excluding its armed enemies from the frontier region. But with whom were the Israelis to deal? The Government of Lebanon, such as it was, was once again being drawn into the orbit of Damascus; the "Army of South Lebanon" was very much the heir to Haddad's militia in terms of both military effectiveness and popular appeal; and the Shi'a inhabitants of southern Lebanon were growing increasingly impatient with the occupation. Its economy badly in need of an overhaul, Israel sought a way out and hinted at the desirabily of U.S. mediation and the sudden suitability of Syria as an interlocutor. Yet Israel's eagerness itself raised questions. Would the U.S., badly burned by its involvement in the process leading to the May 1983 agreement, want to jump back in? Would Syria, presumably for the sake of peace and quiet in Lebanon, be willing to serve, in effect, as the guarantor of Israel's northern frontier? Or would the Asad regime be content to see the Israeli occupation forces bleed for awhile longer? As 1984 drew to a close, Israel's extrication from southern Lebanon was not promising to be an easy process.

NOTES

1. The text of the agreement was printed in The New York Times, 17 May 1983, pp. A12-A13. All quotations of the agreement's text appearing in this chapter are drawn from the Times.

2. Ghassan Tueni, "After the Lebanese-Israeli Agreement," Middle East Insight, Volume Three, No. 1,1983, p. 2.

3. Foreign Broadcast Information Service (FBIS-MEA-84-045), 6 March 1984, p. G1.

4. Foreign Broadcast Information Service (FBIS-MEA-84-048), 10 March 1984, p. I1.

12. Peace for Galilee?

The May 1983 agreement between Lebanon and Israel was but another link in a chain of events involving the Upper Galilee stretching back to World War I. Although the removal of the PLO from southern Lebanon has created an opportunity for stability in the Israel-Lebanon frontier region--an opportunity which the May agreement presumably sought to make palpable--the historical conditions which have made southern Lebanon a battleground in the past have not yet changed.

In 1920 France gave to its Christian clients in Beirut and on Mount Lebanon an enlarged state, a Grand Liban, which included, among other things, a southern region populated mostly by Shi'a Muslims. The failure of France and its clients to create a responsible central administration reflective of a secular sense of Lebanese national identity caused the south to remain essentially ungoverned for over six decades. This failure also left the fragile Lebanese state exposed to the passions and violence generated by the conflict between Zionism and various forms of Arab nationalism, pressures which led to the utter collapse of the state in 1975.

In the wake of Israel's June 1982 invasion there has been much chatter about "reconstituting" the "Lebanese national authority" and "rebuilding" the "Lebanese state." In fact these things never really existed, and their ephemeral nature has nowhere been more evident than in the southern sector of that geographical expression known as Lebanon. France did indeed procure for its clients a portion of Upper Galilee, and did so both to spite Great Britain and expand the Lebanese "nation" to its "historic frontiers." Once in possession of the land, however, the French and their Lebanese friends found the south to be too poor and too Muslim to be worth caring about. The French exacerbated communal tensions by raising a Christian militia in 1925, and slightly more than a decade later they permitted the south to become a sanctuary for Palestinian rebels. Emile Edde, perhaps the most influential Maronite politician of the mandate era, simply wanted to jettison the troublesome area and its people. Unable to get rid of it, and unwilling to govern it, the Lebanese elite permitted the south again to fill up with armed irregulars in the 1970s, an act of negligence which led to the destruction of Lebanon itself.

If the Lebanese elite viewed its southern jurisdiction as a useless appendage, the Zionist leaders saw southern Lebanon first as an opportunity, then as a problem, and again as an opportunity. That the Zionists genuinely wanted the security and water resources of all Upper Galilee to be included within Palestine is beyond dispute. A northern boundary drawn along the Qasimiyah (Litani) River certainly would have been most satisfactory to Dr. Chaim Weizmann. Yet the political leaders of the Jewish community

113

in Palestine, and later Israel, found themselves facing the most galling of circumstances: the Lebanese government, notwithstanding its own indifference toward the people and resources of southern Lebanon, adamantly refused to share those resources with its neighbor to the south. Insult was added to injury when the Litani River was eventually dammed at Qir'awn in order to provide electricity to Beirut, thus leaving a mere trickle for the coveted lower course. Annoyance with Lebanon turned to hostility when Palestinian commandos began to establish bases in southern Lebanon in order to raid the Golan Heights and Israel proper. An Israeli policy of retaliation gradually evolved into one of provocation, as the government began to view the anarchy of southern Lebanon less as a security liability and more as a geopolitical asset. By the late 1970s southern Lebanon had become a pressure point by which Israel, through its own actions or those of its surrogate, Major Haddad, could keep its Palestinian and Syrian enemies thoroughly occupied by destabilizing all of Lebanon. Finally, in 1982, Israel sought to assure the success of its policies in the Occupied Territories by destroying the territorial base of the PLO in southern Lebanon and its political headquarters in Beirut, an action which jeopardized the PLO's political independence and altered the political balance of power in what was left of Lebanon.

Were the Israeli objective simply to seize more territory, to expand the borders of the Jewish State perhaps to the Qasimiyah (Litani) River, this history of Galilee divided would end on a certain note of symmetry: the Zionists, having been frustrated by maladroit British diplomacy and French obstinacy over sixty years ago, bided their time and finally struck in 1982, at long last achieving their cherished goal. Cynics might argue that Israel signed the May 1983 agreement knowing full well that Lebanon would never pull itself together and that Israel would be obliged for security reasons to remain in possession of the south. Surely the tapping of the Litani, perhaps at Lake Qir'awn, would not be long in coming. True, such an annexation would also result in the acquisition of several hundred thousand more troublesome Arabs; an annoyance perhaps, especially considering the Khomeiniites among the Shi'a, but arguably a burden worth the price for achieving the land lost by Lloyd George in 1920.

It is no simple matter to refute conspiracy theories, especially given the byzantine nature of Middle Eastern politics. After all, it is plainly true that conspiracies, large and small, abound in that part of the world. Furthermore, the possibility that Israel will hold onto southern Lebanon cannot be completely ruled out, particularly if the fragmentation of Lebanon becomes definitive. Yet to explain the complex history of the divided Upper Galilee over the past six decades in terms of a conspiratorial land grab seems to simultaneously overstate Israeli objectives and understate their significance. It is conceivable that Israel, having reached the Litani in 1948, could have consolidated its hold in spite of European (especially French) opposition. A convincing pretext probably could have been

invented during the turbulent six days of the June 1967 war.
Surely a move to the Litani during the mid-1970s could have been
explained in terms of defending unarmed Jewish children against
"terrorism." Although the possibility exists that the current
occupation will become permanent, the simple seizure of southern
Lebanon has never been the Zionist style. Instead Israel has
traditionally found itself fascinated with possibilities such as
the normalization of relations with Lebanon, the encouragement of
Maronite separatism, and the destabilizing effects on the PLO and
Syrians resulting from Israeli pressure-point tactics in southern
Lebanon.

There is, therefore, a long history of Lebanese and Israeli
misfeasance, malfeasance, and nonfeasance with regard to southern
Lebanon. Returning to the present, it would appear that three
things need to happen (taking for granted the eventual withdrawal
of all foreign forces) in order for any Lebanon-Israel agreement
to usher in an era of peace for Galilee: the Lebanese government,
whose representative signed the agreement and whose parliament
ratified it, must one day acquire some real authority; it must
assure the effective delivery of governmental services to the
largely Shi'a south; and Israel must do nothing to obstruct either
the creation of a strong central authority in Beirut or its
ability to administer the security region.

For nearly a decade the Lebanese Government has been among
the least relevant institutions in the country. Typically its
writ has extended from the Defense Ministry (whose denizens
included many with ties to the militias) down the street to
Fayadiyah Barracks and down the hill to the Presidential Palace.
At the beginning of 1983 the government more or less controlled
Beirut, although that changed dramatically in early 1984. If this
unstable condition persists reasonable people will one day
conclude that Israel signed an agreement with a corpse. Under
such circumstances Israel would, at a minimum, continue to arm,
train, and advise an indigenous south Lebanon militia capable of
providing early warning to the IDF's Northern Command. Israel
would also feel free (indeed, obligated) to unilaterally prevent
the reintroduction to the frontier region of any armed elements
hostile to Israel.

If a unitary Lebanon emerges, its government will no longer
be able to afford a policy of "benign neglect" toward the south
and the Shi'a community as a whole. Although estimates regarding
the Shi'a share of Lebanon's population vary, it is unanimously
agreed that they now constitute Lebanon's largest sect. The
Lebanese Shi'a are at present disorganized politically: even
AMAL, the most popular of Shi'a organizations, suffers from the
traditional Lebanese malady of rampant localism. Yet given the
massive concentrations of Shi'as in Lebanon's two most volatile
locations--Beirut and the south--it is reasonable to assume that
no viable central authority can exist without broad Shi'a consent.
Therefore, deals must be struck in order to redivide Lebanon's
political and economic pie to the advantage of the Shi'a. Unless

southern Lebanon becomes a place where the government very actively promotes security, education, health, and economic development, it will again become a vacuum to be eventually filled by a variety of armed fanatics: Communists, Khomeiniites, and whatever passes for an Israeli surrogate.

Finally, the utility of any Israel-Lebanon agreement depends on the behavior of Israel. According to David Kimche, Israel wishes to see "a strong central government reasserting its authority over the whole of Lebanon."[1] What is needed is evidence that this statement is more than mere talk. A strong central government is the only kind capable of complying with an agreement. Such a government cannot emerge if Major Haddad's successor, Antoine Lahad, and collaborationist Shi'a militiamen and village guards are permitted to create alternatives to the official government. The question posed in the preceding chapter -- i.e., is Israel now interested in security matters of a défensive nature instead of pressure point tactics--will be answered by actual Israeli policies regarding the establishment of central authority in Lebanon. In the long run, unless Israel is willing to assume complete responsibility for the economic and political aspirations of the volatile Lebanese Shi'a community in the south, there will be no peace for Galilee without a real government for Lebanon. Reliance on hired hands, whose numbers inevitably swell with social misfits and ne'er-do-wells, can only lead to the kind of widespread turbulence and violence that may once again oblige Israeli Galileans to live in bomb shelters while Lebanese Galileans die in large numbers.

Ironically, therefore, the prospects for peace in Galilee may well depend on the one element which has been routinely ignored for over sixty years: the people of southern Lebanon. It is only through their willing cooperation that "good neighbourly relations" and "good fences" will become realities.

NOTES

1. David Kimche, "Lebanon, The Hour of Truth," Middle East Insight, Volume Three, No.1, 1983, p.7.

Bibliography

Abu-Izzeddin, Halim Said, ed. Lebanon and its Provinces: A Study by the Governors of the Five Provinces. Beirut: Khayats, 1963.

Abu Lughod, Janet. "Demographic Transformation." In The Transformation of Palestine, pp. 139-163. Edited by Ibrahim Abu Lughod. Evanston: Northwestern University Press, 1971.

Agreement Between His Majesty's Government and the French Government Respecting the Boundary Line Between Syria and Palestine from the Mediterranean to El Hamme. Cmd. 1910. London: His Majesty's Stationery Office, 1923.

Agreement Between Palestine and Syria and the Lebanon to Facilitate Good Neighbourly Relations in Connection With Frontier Questions. London: His Majesty's Stationery Office, 1927.

Alan, Ray. "Lebanon: Israel's Friendliest Neighbor." Commentary (June 1952): 551-559.

Alexander, Yonah and Nicholas N. Kittrie, eds. Crescent and Star: Arab & Israeli Perspectives on the Middle East Conflict. New York: AMS Press, Inc., 1972.

Anderson, Jack. "Terrorist Wages One-Man War Against Israel." Washington Post, 25 April 1983.

An-Nahar Arab Report & Memo. 28 August 1978, p. 4.

Arab Report and Record. March-July 1978.

Area Handbook for Lebanon. Washington: U.S. Government Printing Office, 1974.

Aronsfeld, C. C. "The Historical Boundaries of Palestine." Contemporary Review 213 (December 1968): 289-297.

Bar-Yaacov, N. The Israeli-Syrian Armistice. Jerusalem: Magnes Press, 1967.

Bar-Zohar, Michael. Ben Gurion: The Armed Prophet. Englewood Cliffs: Prentice-Hall, Inc., 1968.

Beaumont, Peter, Gerald H. Blake and Malcolm Wagstaff, eds. The Middle East: A Geographical Survey. London: John Wiley & Sons, 1976.

Berger, Earl. The Covenant and the Sword. London: Routledge & Kegan Paul Ltd., 1965.

Bochenski, Feliks and William Diamond. William. "TVA's in the Middle East." Middle East Journal 4 (January 1950): 52-82.

Boggs, S. Whittemore. International Boundaries--A Study of Boundary Functions and Problems. New York: Columbia University Press, 1940.

117

118

Brawer, Moshe. "The Geographical Background of the Jordan Water Dispute." In
Essays in Political Geography, pp. 225-242. Edited by Charles A. Fisher.
London: Methuen & Co. Ltd., 1968.

Brecher, Michael. Decisions in Israel's Foreign Policy. New Haven: Yale
University Press, 1975.

Bull, Odd. War and Peace in the Middle East. London: Leo
Cooper, 1976.

Burns, Lieutenant General E. L. M. Between Arab and Israeli. London: George
G. Harrap & Co., Ltd., 1962.

Bushinsky, Jay. "Lebanese Major Shows Israelis His Touchy Position."
Christian Science Monitor, 11 October 1977, p. 10.

Carlson, Lucile. Geography and World Politics. Englewood Cliffs: Prentice-
Hall, 1958.

Cemal, Pasa. Memories of a Turkish Statesman. London: Hutchinson & Co.,
1922.

Childers, Erskine B. "The Wordless Wish: From Citizens to Refugees." In The
Transformation of Palestine, pp. 165-202. Edited by Ibrahim Abu Lughod.
Evanston: Northwestern University Press, 1971.

Cobban, Helena. "Pacifying South Lebanon Tied to Israeli Cooperation."
Christian Science Monitor, 19 August 1977, p. 4.

_____. "S. Lebanon: Integration with Israel?" Christian Science Monitor,
9 November 1977, p. 34.

Cohen, Aharon. Israel and the Arab World. New York: Funk & Wagnalls, 1970.

Cooke, Hedley V. Challenge and Response in the Middle East: The Quest for
Prosperity, 1919-1951. New York: Harper & Brothers, 1951.

Cooley, John K. Green March, Black September. London: Frank Cass, 1973.

_____. "Lebanon Fears Loss of Water to Israel." Christian Science Monitor,
23 March 1978, p. 3.

_____. "PLO-Israeli Strife Shakes Uneasy Peace in Lebanon." Christian
Science Monitor, 7 April 1978, p. 4.

_____. "UN Faces an Uncertain Role in South Lebanon." Christian Science
Monitor, 22 March 1978, p. 34.

Cressey, George B. Crossroads: Land and Life in Southwest Asia. Chicago: J.
B. Lippencott Company, 1960.

Cumming, Henry H. Franco-British Rivalry in the Post-War Near East; the

<u>Decline of French Influence</u>. New York: Oxford University Press, 1938.

Dane, Edmund. <u>British Campaigns in the Nearer East, 1914-1918</u>. London: Hodder and Stoughton, 1917-1919. 2V.

<u>Documents on British Foreign Policy 1919-39, First Series Volume I 1919</u>. Edited by E. L. Woodward and Rohan Butler. London: His Majesty's Stationery Office, 1947.

<u>Documents on British Foreign Policy 1919-39, First Series Volume IV 1919</u>. Edited by E. L. Woodward and Rohan Butler. London: His Majesty's Stationery Office, 1952.

<u>Documents on British Foreign Policy 1919-39, First Series Volume VII 1920</u>. Edited by Rohan Butler and J. P. T. Bury. London: Her Majesty's Stationery Office, 1958.

<u>Documents on British Foreign Policy 1919-39, First Series Volume VIII 1920</u>. Edited by Rohan Butler and J. P. T. Bury. London: Her Majesty's Stationery Office, 1963.

Edde, Jacques. <u>Geographie Liban-Syrie</u>. Beyrouth: Imprimerie Catholique, 1941.

<u>Facts on File</u>, 21 April 1978, pp. 274-275.

Falls, Cyril. <u>Armageddon: 1918</u>. Philadelphia: J. B. Lippincott Company, 1964.

Faris, Basim A. <u>Electric Power in Syria and Palestine</u>. Beirut: American University of Beirut, 1936.

Farmer, Leslie. "The Beleaguered Litani." <u>Mid East</u> X (February 1970): 15-20.

Fisher, Sidney Nettleton. <u>The Middle East: A History</u>. New York: Alfred A. Knopf, 1969.

Fisher, W. B. <u>The Middle East: A Physical, Social and Regional Geography</u>. London: Methuen & Co., 1971.

<u>Franco-British Convention of December 23, 1920, on Certain Points Connected with the Mandates for Syria and the Lebanon, Palestine and Mesopotamia</u>. Cmd. 1195. London: His Majesty's Stationery Office, 1921.

Frischwaser-Ra'anan, H. F. <u>The Frontiers of a Nation</u>. London: The Batchworth Press, 1955.

George-Samne, Dr. <u>La Syrie</u>. Paris: Editions Bossard, 1920.

Godsell, Geoffrey. "Israeli Retaliation Raids Buffet U.S. Peace Efforts." <u>Christian Science Monitor</u>, 10 November 1977, pp. 1, 11.

Goodman, Hirsh. "IDF Extends its Control of Southern Lebanon." Jerusalem Post (International Edition), 21 March 1978, pp. 1-2.

_____. "Israel Forces Holding Southern Lebanon." Jerusalem Post (International Edition), 21 March 1978, p. 7.

_____. "Israel 'Guidelines' for Lebanese Troops." Jerusalem Post (International Edition), 1 August 1978, pp. 1-2.

_____. "Muddling Along in Lebanon." Jerusalem Post (International Edition), 15 August 1978, p. 8.

Grose, Peter. "Arabs Ejected from Homes in '48 May Not Return." New York Times, 24, July 1972, p. 2.

Hagopian, Elaine and Samih Farsoun, eds. South Lebanon. Detroit: Association of Arab-American University Graduates, Inc., August 1978.

Himadeh, Sa'id B., ed. Economic Organization of Syria. Beirut: American University of Beirut, 1936.

Hirsch, Abraham H. "Utilization of International Rivers in the Middle East." American Journal of International Law 50 (January 1956): 81-100.

Hitti, Philip K. Lebanon in History: From the Earliest times to the Present. New York: St. Martin's Press, 1967.

Hourani, A. H. Syria and Lebanon: A Political Essay. London: Oxford University Press, 1946.

Howard, Harry N. The Partition of Turkey: A Diplomatic History, 1913-23. Norman: University of Oklahoma Press, 1931.

Howe, Marvine. "Israelis Said to be Seeking Use of Lebanese Villages." New York Times, 26 February 1978, p. 11.

_____. "PLO Reports Raid on Israeli Troops." New York Times, 26 March 1978, p. 10.

Hudson, James. "The Litani River of Lebanon: An Example of Middle Eastern Water Development." Middle East Journal 25 (Winter 1971): 1-14.

Hudson, Michael. "Fedayeen are Forcing Lebanon's Hand. Mid East X (February 1970): 7-14.

_____. The Palestinian Factor in the Lebanese Civil War." Middle East Journal 32 (Summer 1978): 261-278.

Hurewitz, J. C. Diplomacy in the Near and Middle East. A Documentary Record: 1914-1956. Volume II. Princeton: D. Van Nostrand Company, Inc., 1956.

Ingrams, Doreen. _Palestine Papers 1917-1922: Seeds of Conflict._ London: John Murray, 1972.

"Israel Leaves Southern Lebanon." _Christian Science Monitor_, 14 June 1978, p. 3.

Israel's Occupation of Palestine and Other Arab Territories. Chicago: Association of Arab-American University Graduates, Inc., July 1970.

Issawi, Charles. "Economic Development and Liberalism in Lebanon." _Middle East Journal_ 18 (Summer 1964): 279-292.

Jerusalem Domestic Service, 21 March 1978. Cited in Foreign Broadcast Information Service (FBIS-MEA-78-56) 22 March 1978, p. N3.

Jureidini, Paul A. and William E. Hazen, _The Palestinian Movement in Politics_. Lexington: D.C. Heath and Company, 1976.

Karmon, Yehuda. _Israel: A Regional Geography._ London: Wiley-Interscience, 1971.

_____. "The Drainage of the Huleh Swamps." _Geographical Review_, April 1960: 169-193.

Keesing's Contemporary Archives, 23 December 1977.

Keith, Kenneth J. "Succession to Bilateral Treaties by Seceding States." _American Journal of International Law_ 61 (April 1967): 521-546.

Khanzadian, Z. _Atlas de Geographie Economique de Syrie et du Liban._ Paris: L. de Bertalot, 1926.

Kimche, David. "Lebanon: The Hour of Truth." _Middle East Insight_, Vol. 3 No. 1 (May-July 1983): 4-7.

Kirk, George. _Survey of International Affairs: The Middle East 1945-1950._ London: Oxford University Press, 1954.

_____. _The Middle East in the War. Survey of International Affairs 1939-1943_. Volume 6. London: Oxford University Press, 1952.

Kishtainy, Khalid. _Whither Israel? A Study of Zionist Expansionism_. Beirut: Palestine Liberation Organization Research Center, 1970.

Kurzman, Dan. _Genesis 1948_. Cleveland: The New American Library, Inc., 1970.

Laqueur, Walter. _A History of Zionism._ New York: Holt, Rinehart, Winston, 1972.

"Lebanese Army is Set to Stop War in South." _New York Times_, 11 September 1977, p. 14.

"Lebanese Can Learn a Trade in Israel." Jerusalem Post (International Edition), 14 February 1978, p. 4.

"Lebanese Claim for Equal Wages." Jerusalem Post (International Edition), 21 February 1978, p. 4.

Le Figaro (Paris), 20 April 1978, p. 16. Cited in Foreign Broadcast Information Service (FBIS-MEA-78-79), 24 April 1978, p. G4.

Lloyd George, David. The Truth About the Peace Treaties. London: Victor Gollancz Ltd., 1938.

Longrigg, Stephen Hemsley. Syria and Lebanon Under French Mandate. London: Oxford University Press, 1958.

Lorch, Lt. Col. Natanel. The Edge of the Sword: Israel's War of Independence, 1947-9. New York: G. P. Putnam's Sons, 1961.

Markham, James M. "Syria's Role in Lebanon is Murkier than Ever." New York Times, 26 March 1978, p. 2E.

_____. "The War that Won't Go Away." New York Times Magazine, 9 October 1977, pp. 33-passim (52).

Marlowe, John. The Seat of Pilate: An Account of the Palestine Mandate. London: The Cresset Press, 1959.

Mehdi, Mohammad Taki. "Arab-Israeli Tension: A Study of Border Conflicts." Berkeley: University of California, 1953. Unpublished thesis.

Meinertzhagen, Colonel Richard. Middle East Diary 1917-1956. New York: Thomas Yoseloff, 1960.

Mohr, Charles. "Lebanese Border with Israel Calm." New York Times, 7 November 1969, p. 5.

Moore, John Norton, ed. The Arab-Israeli Conflict. Volume III: Documents. Princeton: Princeton University Press, 1974.

Morris, Jason. "Shakey Truce Invites Israeli Troops Again." Christian Science Monitor, 17 October 1977, p. 7.

Mosley, Leonard. Gideon Goes to War. New York: Charles Scribner's Sons, 1955.

Moughrabi, Fuad and Naseer Aruri, eds. Lebanon: Crisis and Challenge in the Arab World. Detroit: Association of Arab-American University Graduates, January 1977.

Nevakivi, Jukka. Britain, France and the Arab Middle East 1914-1920. London: The Athlone Press, 1969.

"New Government, Old Problems." An-Nahar Arab Report & Memo, 24 April 1978, pp. 2-3.

Newsweek, 27 March, 3 April 1978.

New York Times, 7 November 1949, 21 June 1967, 15 April 1976, 1 February 1977, 11 September 1977, 29 October 1977, 17 May 1983.

"Not Just a Tiny Strip of Land" (Survey on Lebanon) Economist, 26 January 1974.

O'Ballance, Edgar. Arab Guerrilla Power 1967-72. Hamden: Anchor Books. 1974.

_____. The Arab-Israeli War, 1948. London: Faber and Faber Limited, 1956.

Ofner, Francis. "Lebanon Christians Block Army Drive." Christian Science Monitor, 1 August 1978, pp. 1, 10.

Orni, Efraim and Elisha Efrat, Geography of Israel. Philadelphia: The Jewish Publication Society of America, 1971.

Peretz, Don. "Development of the Jordan Valley Waters." Middle East Journal 9 (Autumn 1955): 397-412.

_____. "River Schemes and Their Effect on Economic Development in Jordan, Syria and Lebanon." Middle East Journal 18 (Summer 1964): 293-305.

Pichon, Jean. Le Partage du Proche-Orient. Paris: J. Peyronnet & Cie., 1938.

Playfair, Major General I. S. O. The Mediterranean and the Middle East, Volume II. History of the Second World War. United Kingdom Military Series. Edited by J. R. M. Butler. London: Her Majesty's Stationery Office, 1956.

Prescott, J. R. V. The Geography of Frontiers and Boundaries. Chicago: Aldine Publishing Company, 1965.

_____. Political Geography. London: Methuen & Co., Ltd., 1972.

"Press Conference with Ezer Weizman & Mordechai Gur." Jerusalem Domestic Service, 20 March 1978. Cited in Foreign Broadcast Information Service (FBIS-MEA-78-55) 21 March 1978, pp. N3-N5.

Quandt, William B., Fuad Jabber, Ann Mosely Lesch. The Politics of Palestinian Nationalism. Berkeley: University of California Press, 1973.

Ralphaeli, N. "Development Planning: Lebanon." Western Political Quarterly XX (September 1967): 714-728.

Ruedy, John. "Dynamics of Land Alienation." In The Transformation of Palestine, pp. 119-138. Edited by Ibrahim Abu Lughod. Evanston: Northwestern

University Press, 1971.

Sachar, Howard M. A History of Israel: From the Rise of Zionism to Our Time. New York: Alfred A. Knopf, 1976.

_____. The Emergence of the Middle East: 1914-24. New York: Alfred A. Knopf, 1969.

Sacher, H., ed. Zionism and the Jewish Future. New York: The MacMillan Company, 1916.

Sacher, Harry. Israel: The Establishment of a State. New York: British Book Centre, 1952.

Safadi, Anan. Jerusalem Post Magazine, 7 April 1978, p. 4.

Saliba, Samir N. The Jordan River Dispute. The Hague: Martinus Nijhoff, 1968.

Salibi, Kamal S. Crossroads to Civil War: Lebanon 1958-1976. Delmar: Caravan Books, 1976.

_____. The Modern History of Lebanon. New York: Federick A. Praeger, Publishers, 1965.

Samuel, Herbert. Palestine. Report of the High Commissioner on the Administration of Palestine, 1920-1925. London: His Majesty's Stationery Office, 1925.

Samuels, Gertrude. "Israel's New 'Experiment in Peace.'" New Leader, 27 September 1976, pp. 9-11.

Schmidt, Dana Adams. "Prospects for a Solution of the Jordan River Valley Dispute." Middle Eastern Affairs VI (January 1955): 1-12.

Segev, Shemu'el. Tel Aviv Ha'arez. 12 April 1978. Cited in Foreign Broadcast Information Service (FBIS-MEA-78-72) 13 April 1978, p. N5.

Sharif, Hassan. "South Lebanon. Its History and Geopolitics." In South Lebanon, pp. 9-34. Edited by Elaine Hagopian and Samih Farsoun. Detroit: Association of Arab-American University Graduates, Inc., August 1978.

Shimoni, Yaacov and Evyatar Levine, eds. Political Dictionary of the Middle East in the 20th Century. New York: Quadrangle, 1974.

Shorrock, William I. French Imperialism in the Middle East: The Failure of Policy in Syria and Lebanon 1900-1914. Madison: The University of Wisconsin Press, 1976.

Smith, George Adams, ed. Atlas of the Historical Geography of the Holy Land. London: Hodder and Stoughton, 1915.

Smith, Terence. "Israel Builds New Border Fence." New York Times, 14 July 1974, pp. 1, 17.

_____. Israelis Stepping up Patrols in Lebanon." New York Times, 3 August 1976, pp. 1, 17.

Sobel, Lester A., ed. Palestinian Impasse: Arab Guerrillas & International Terror. New York: Facts on File, Inc., 1977.

State of Israel Government Yearbook 5712 (1951/52). Jerusalem: Government Printer, 1951.

Statement of the Zionist Organisation Regarding Palestine. 3 February 1919.

Stein, Leonard. The Balfour Declaration. New York: Simon and Schuster, 1961.

"Syria Has an Enemy Within." New York Times, 4 September 1977, Section 4, p. 2.

Tanner, Henry. "In South Lebanon, an Odd War: Arab Soldiers with Israeli Arms." New York Times, 8 October 1976, pp. 1, 7.

Taylor, Alan R. Prelude to Israel; An Analysis of Zionist Diplomacy, 1897-1947. New York: Philosophical Library, 1959.

Temperley, H. W. V., ed. A History of the Peace Conference of Paris. Volume II. London: Henry Frowde and Hodder & Stoughton, 1924.

Thicknesse, S. G. Arab Refugees: A Survey of Resettlement Possibilities. London: Royal Institute of International Affairs, 1949.

Times (London). 2 May, 28 May, 1 July, 26 July, 10 October 1938; 4 May 1939; 17 January 1949.

Toynbee, Arnold J., ed. Survey of International Affairs 1925. Volume I. London: Oxford University Press, 1927.

Tueni, Ghassan. "After the Lebanese-Israeli Agreement." Middle East Insight, Vol. 3 No. 1 (May-July 1983): 2-3.

Vilnay, Zev. The New Israel Atlas. Bible to Present Day. Jerusalem: Israel Universities Press, 1968.

Weinberger, Naomi Joy. "Peacekeeping Options in Lebanon." Middle East Journal, Vol. 37 No. 3 (Summer 1983): 341-369.

Weizmann, Chaim. Trial and Error, The Autobiography of Chaim Weizmann. New York: Harper & Brothers, 1949.

Wiznitzer, Louis. "UN Troops Sitting on a 'Volcano' Now That the Israelis Have Pulled Out." Christian Science Monitor, 15 June 1978, p. 6.

Zamir, Meir. "Emile Edde and the Territorial Integrity of Lebanon." Middle Eastern Studies 14 (May 1978): 232-235.

Zeine, Zeine N. The Struggle of Arab Independence. Beirut: Khayat's, 1960.

Index

Acco. <u>See</u> Acre
Acre (Israel), 3, 4-5(figs.),
  7, 8(fig.), 11, 12(fig.),
  17, 18(fig.), 51, 53, 63
 Arab population, 48
 as frontier region, 19, 47
Acre Plain, 18(fig.)
ADL. <u>See</u> Armistice Demarcation
 Line
Al Khiyan (Lebanon), 82, 83,
 91
Allenby, Edmund, 7, 11, 23, 43
Allon, Yigal, 38, 80
Al 'Udaysah (Lebanon), 53
Amal organization, 99, 100,
 115
American University (Beirut),
 30
Anglo-French Convention (1923),
 3, 14, 17, 29, 30, 39, 107
An Naqura (Lebanon), 99
Antwerp (Belgium) bus attack,
 101
Arab Deterrent Forces, 82
Arab economic boycott, 63
Arab-Israeli war
 1948, 20, 30, 31, 38, 51, 53-59
 1956, 67
 1967, 29, 36, 37, 38, 66-67,
 68, 71, 115
Arab League, 33, 36, 37, 82
 Political Committee, 35
Arab Liberation Army, 53, 55
Arabs
 Damascus-based, 1
 nationalism, 45, 46, 48, 113
 <u>See also</u> <u>Fedayeen</u> commando
  activity; Palestine, Arab

uprisings; Upper Galilee,
 population
Arafat, Yasir, 91, 98, 99, 100,
 101, 102
Argov, Shlomo, 101
Armistice Demarcation Line (ADL),
 56-57, 58(fig.), 59, 63, 64,
 65, 68
Arqub (Lebanon), 18(fig.), 73.
 <u>See also</u> Hermon, Mount
Ar Rashidiyah (Lebanon), 83
Assad, Hafez, 79, 85(n15), 92,
 97, 110
Athens airport. <u>See</u> Israeli air-
 liner attack
<u>Atlas of the Historical Geo-
 graphy of the Holy Land</u>
 (Smith), 11, 13
At Tayibah (Lebanon), 87, 88
Australian Division, 49-50
Awwali River, 6(fig.), 10(fig.),
 12(fig.), 18(fig.), 34, 107
Ayn Dara (Lebanon), 101

Balat (Israel), 57
Balfour Declaration (1917), 3
Banat Ya'qub Bridge, 31, 35
Banias (Syria), 8(fig.), 9,
 10(fig.), 14
Banias River, 38
 diversion plan, 35, 36
Bar'am (Israel), 61-62(n44)
Baruk area (Lebanon), 106(fig.),
 107
Bar-Yaacov, N., 36
Beaufort Castle, 97
Beersheba. <u>See</u> "Dan to
 Beersheba"

Rosh Pinna Sill, 18(fig.)
Russia, 3

Sabotage. See Fedayeen commando
  activity; Israel, retaliation
  policy; Palestine Liberation
  Organization
Sabra refugee camp (Lebanon),
  102
SAC. See Israeli-Lebanese
  Security Arrangements
  Committee
Sachar, Howard M., 23, 53
Sadr, Musa(imam), 99
Safed (Israel), 4-5(figs.), 7,
  8(fig.), 17, 30
 Arab population, 48
 frontier, 19, 47
Saida. See Sidon
Saliba, Samir N., 31
Salibi, Kamal S., 71
Saliha, 51
Samaria, 11
Sarkis, Elias, 81, 82, 83, 91,
  92
Security Arrangements Super-
  vision Centers, 109, 110
Security belt, 89, 90, 91, 92,
  97
Security zones (1983), 106(fig.),
  107-109
Shab'a (Lebanon), 68
Shamir (Israel), 75
Shamir, Yitzhak, 111
Sharif, Hasan, 48
Shatila refugee camp
  (Lebanon), 102
Shelomi (Israel), 61-62(n44)
Shi'ite Muslims, 21, 25, 27(n7),
  33, 81, 84, 88, 90, 99, 111,
  113, 115, 116
 Khomeiniites, 114
Shtawra Agreement (1977),
  82, 83
Shuf region (Lebanon), 101
Sidon (Lebanon), 6, 8(fig.),
  10(fig.), 12(fig.), 18(fig.),
  30, 100, 106(fig.), 107
 Sunnis in, 27(n7)
Siilasvuo, 89
Sinai Peninsula, 7, 36, 38, 66,
  98
Smith, Adam, 11, 13
Smuggling, 20, 65

Soleh Boneh, Ltd. (Haifa), 46
Spicer, R.G.B., 46
Stone of Wisdom operation, 88,
  90
Suez Canal, 7, 23, 24
Sunni Muslims, 27(n7)
Sykes-Picot Agreement (1916),
  3, 7
 Line, 5(fig.), 9, 11
Syria, 20
 and Arab nationalism, 46, 48
 army, 82
 and fedayeen forces, 71, 72,
  73, 74, 79, 81, 83
 and Israel, 31, 37, 49, 56, 57,
  64, 66, 67, 79, 80, 98, 101,
  111, 115
 in 1919 (map), 8(fig.)
 Ottoman governor, 7
 Palestinian boundary, 6(fig.),
  10(fig.), 14, 19, 27(n1),
  44(fig.), 46, 47
 See also Banias River; Good
  Neighborly Relations Accord;
  under France; Lebanon

Tarshiya (Israel), 58(fig.)
Tegart, Sir Charles, 46
Tegart's Wall, 46-47, 48, 50
Tel Aviv (Israel), 30
Tel Hai, 1, 11, 43
Terrorism. See Fedayeen
  commando activity; Israel,
  retaliation policy; Israel-
  Lebanon agreement
Thatcher, Margaret, 101
Tiberias, Lake, 3, 4-5(figs.),
  18(fig.), 27(n1), 31, 35
Tibnin (Lebanon), 92
Transjordan, 46
Trumpeldor, Joseph, 1
Tueni, Ghassan, 105
Turkey, 3
Tyre (Lebanon), 4-6(figs.),
  8(fig.), 10(fig.), 12(fig.),
  17, 18(fig.), 30, 89,
  106(fig.)
 frontier, 19
 Sunnis in, 27(n7)
Tyre Pocket. See under Palestine
  Liberation Organization
Tyre Valley, 18(fig.)